Ancient Apostles

WRITTEN FOR
THE DESERET SUNDAY SCHOOL UNION

By

David O. McKay

General Superintendent

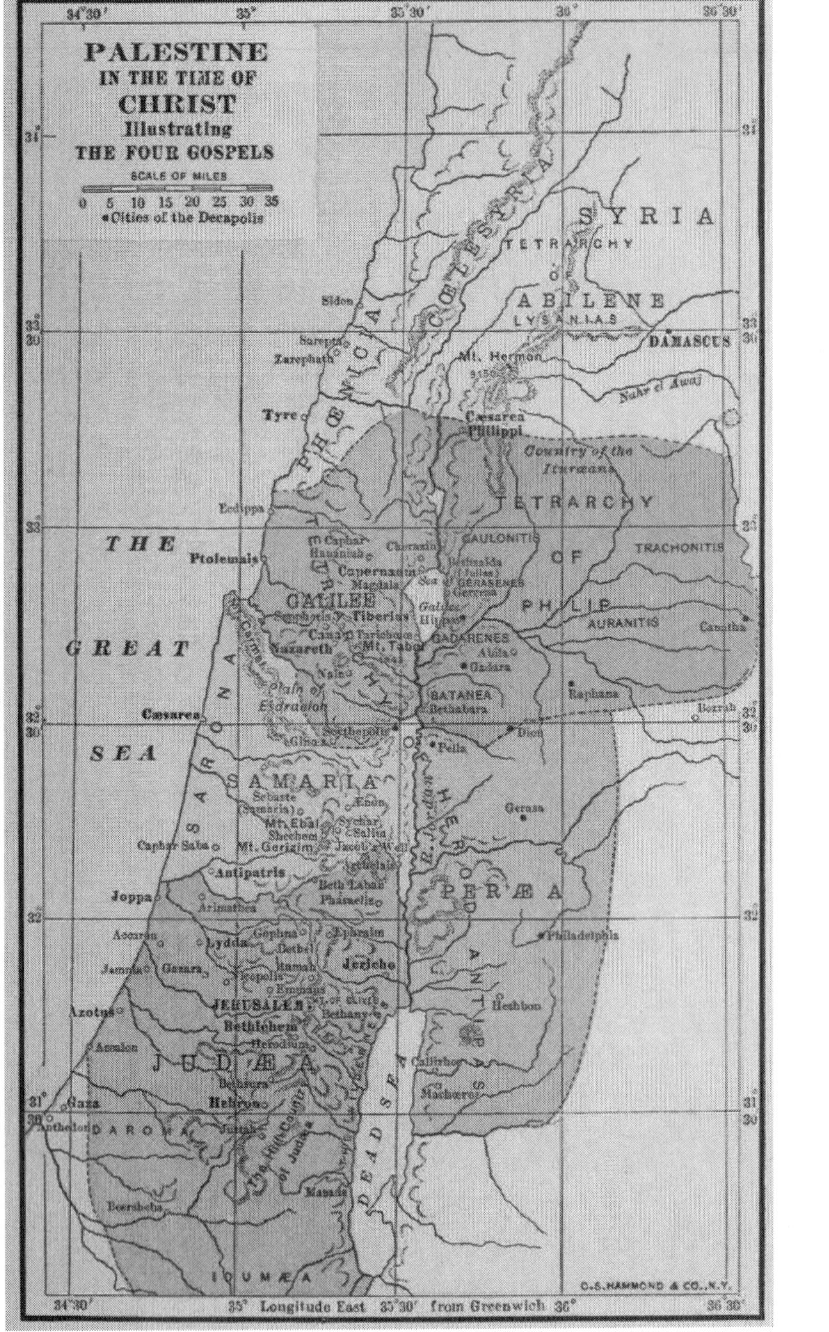
PALESTINE
IN THE TIME OF
CHRIST
Illustrating
THE FOUR GOSPELS
SCALE OF MILES
0 5 10 15 20 25 30 35
• Cities of the Decapolis
SYRIA
TETRARCHY
OF
ABILENE
LYSANIAS
DAMASCUS
Sidon
Sarepta
Zarephath
Mt. Hermon
Nahr el Awaj
Tyre
Cæsarea
Philippi
Country of the
Ituræans
TETRARCHY
OF
PHILIP
Ecdippa
THE
GREAT
SEA
Ptolemais
Capernaum
Magdala
Chorazin
GAULONITIS
TRACHONITIS
GALILEE
Tiberias
Cana
Nazareth
Mt. Tabor
Nain
GADARENES
Abila
Gadara
AURANITIS
Canatha
Plain of
Esdraelon
BATANEA
Bethabara
Raphana
Bozrah
Cæsarea
Scythopolis
Pella
Dion
SAMARIA
Sebaste
(Samaria)
Ænon
Mt. Ebal
Shechem
Sychar
Salim
Mt. Gerizim
Jacob's Well
Caphar Saba
Gerasa
Antipatris
Joppa
Beth Laban
Phasaelis
PERÆA
Arimathea
Accaron
Lydda
Gophna
Bethel
Ephraim
Philadelphia
Jamnia
Gazara
Ramah
Jericho
Emmaus
Azotus
JERUSALEM
Bethany
Bethlehem
Heshbon
Ascalon
Herodium
JUDÆA
Callirhoe
Bethzura
Machærus
Gaza
Hebron
Anthedon
DAROMA
Juttah
DEAD SEA
Masada
Beersheba
IDUMÆA
C.S. HAMMOND & CO., N.Y.
Longitude East from Greenwich

Contents

PREFACE

"Ancient Apostles" is written as one of the series of text books prepared for use in the Sunday Schools of the Church of Jesus Christ of Latter-day Saints. Its purpose is to give a simple account of the leading incidents in the lives of the chief Apostles of Christ in the Holy Land, with the view of developing faith in the hearts of the children in the principles of the Gospel, and in the divine organization of the Church.

Prominent traits of character in the different disciples are pointed out as the circumstances in the lessons permit. These should be so emphasized in the presentation to the class that the pupils will be led not only to appreciate them as commendable and emulative, but to realize that by personal exertion all these good traits may become theirs. Virtuous and honorable actions are the stones by which we build the mansion of character.

Each chapter is planned, also, to emphasize one general aim, which should be correlated with the incident or incidents with which the personality of the Apostle and his companions is associated. Since it is difficult, if not impossible to teach morality and doctrine without personality, the wise teachers will ever keep in mind that the persons, settings, actions, and conversations in this little work are only a means of teaching truths and principles of conduct that will contribute to the moulding of God-like character in their boys and girls.

The suggestive outlines and aims in the appendix are offered as helps and guides to teachers. Only a few suggestive *applications* are offered; but no lesson should be given, or even prepared, without the teachers attempting, at least, to devise the most efficient means of introducing into the children's daily lives the aims and ideals taught.

The sincere wish of the author is that at least part of the pleasure experienced in writing these lessons may be realized by those who prepare to teach them, and by those who read them, and that their studious efforts through the blessings of the Lord, will bring to them that peace and satisfaction which come with the realization of having helped to make better and more efficient the men and women of tomorrow.

CHRIST'S CHARGE TO PETER.

PART ONE—PETER.
LESSON 1 "LIGHT-FOUNTAINS"

"No man has come to true greatness who has not felt in some degree that his life belongs to his race, and that what God gives him He gives him for mankind."

"If any man seek for greatness, let him forget greatness and ask for truth, and he will find both."

"Nothing can make a man truly great but being truly good, and partaking of God's holiness."

Influence of Great Men.

Everybody likes to read and to hear about great men. Children, and grown people, too, delight to learn how the leaders of men in the past have made the world better and happier by their noble deeds. And when, after many years have passed, people still see how much good those leaders of men did in the world, worthy aspirations are awakened, and boys and girls of today desire to emulate the lives of these heroes of the past; for, as the poet Longfellow says:

"Lives of great men all remind us
We can make our lives sublime;
And, departing, leave behind us
Footprints on the sands of time."

Boy's Ideals.

Every boy has somebody who becomes his ideal. Or perhaps there are more than one who form this ideal—one man, for instance, might be a good athlete, and the boy wishes to be just like him; another is a good violinist, and the boy feels that he, too, would some day like to be a musician; another is an able speaker, and the boy desires some day to be a great orator. But, sometimes, boys, and girls, too, for that matter, choose bad men for their ideals. This happens when young folks read trashy books or associate with trashy or evil-minded men. How unfortunate that little boy is who happens to read or to hear about some highwayman or robber, and has awakened in his young mind a desire to be like that bad man! How unfortunate for the boy who chooses for his ideal a man who smokes, and drinks and swaggers through life in idleness!

Sign Posts.

Thus we see that the lives of men become sign posts to us, pointing the way along roads that lead either to lives of usefulness and happiness or to lives of selfishness and misery. It is important, then, that we seek, both in life and in books, the companionship of the best and noblest men and women. Carlyle, a great English writer, says that "Great men taken up in any way are profitable company. We cannot look, however imperfectly, upon a great man, without gaining something by him. He is the living 'light-fountain,' which it is good and pleasant to be near."

Secret of Greatness.

If you will study the lives of these great "light-fountains" of the world, you will learn of at least one thing that has made their names endure. It is this: Each one has given something of his life to make the world better. They did not spend all their time seeking only pleasure and ease, and a "good time" for themselves alone, but found their greatest joy in making others happy and more comfortable. All such good deeds live forever, even though the world may never hear of them.

How Some Have Failed.

There is an old, old story that a man from another planet was permitted to visit this earth. From a high mountain peak, he looked down upon the busy towns and cities of the world. Millions of men, like ants, were busy building palaces of pleasure, and other things that would not last. As he left to go back, he said, "All these people are spending their time in building just birds' nests. No wonder they fail and are ashamed."

How the Truly Great Have Built.

All the truly great men of the world have built something besides "birds' nests." Out of the deep longing of their minds and hearts, they have brought forth gems of truth that have made the world richer. They have wrought deeds of love and sacrifice that have inspired millions. In so doing, they might have suffered; many indeed have met untimely death; but all who thus gave their lives, saved them. That which we do for God and our fellowmen lives forever; that which we do just for ourselves cannot endure.

"To have sown in the souls of men
  One thought that will not die—
To have been a link in the chain of life
  Shall be immortality."

Lincoln.

When we hear anything about a great man we want to know everything about him—where he was born, who his parents were, where he lived, how he played, with whom he played, in what kind of house he lived, where he went in swimming, where he fished, etc., etc. Such things about George Washington and Abraham Lincoln, for example, are always interesting. What boy is there who doesn't like to hear about the poor boy Lincoln in the little log cabin in the backwoods of Indiana; to picture him there among the bears and other wild animals; to picture him sitting by the fireplace learning to cipher by using a piece of charcoal on a wooden shovel because he had no slate, no paper or lead pencil! Abraham Lincoln was a great and good man, and we want to know everything about him even when he was a boy, partly to help us become somewhat like him; for, as Lincoln wrote,

> "Good boys who to their books apply,
> Will all be great men by and by."

Little Known of Apostles' Boyhood.

Unfortunately, we know very little about the boyhood days of the Ancient Apostles, about whom we shall read in this little book. It is true we can partly judge of what kind of boys they were by the kind of men they became; but the little incidents of childhood and youth, which tended to mould their character, and in which we now would be so interested, though nineteen hundred years have passed, were never written, and may never be known. They grew to manhood before the opportunity came for them to render that service to the world which has made their names immortal.

Most Favored Men.

In one respect, however, they were the most favored men the world has known, because they had the privilege of associating daily—almost hourly, for about two and one-half years, with the Savior of the world. No wonder, then, that they became great, when they had such an example of true Greatness constantly before them. As soon as they learned to love Jesus, they desired to be like Him, and so remembered His teachings, and tried to do as He said. Surely it will be good for us to get acquainted with such men.

Why Apostles Are Known.

Just think! The only reason the world knows anything about them is because having met the Savior, they made Him their guide in life. If they hadn't, nobody now would know that such men had ever lived. They would have lived and died and been forgotten just as thousands of other men in their day lived and died and nobody knows or cares anything about them; just as thousands and thousands are living today, wasting their time and energy in useless living, choosing the wrong kind of men for their ideals, turning their footsteps into the road of Pleasure and Indulgence instead of the road of Service. Soon they will reach the end of their journey in life, and nobody can say that the world is any better for their having lived in it. At the close of each day such men leave their pathway as barren as they found it—they plant no trees to give shade to others, nor rosebushes to make the world sweeter and brighter to those who follow—no kind deeds, no noble service—just a barren, unfruitful, desert-like pathway, strewn, perhaps, with thorns and thistles.

Not so with the disciples who chose Jesus for their Guide. Their lives are like gardens of roses from which the world may pluck beautiful flowers forever.

LESSON 2 Early Life and Surroundings

"It is with youth as with plants, from the first fruits they bear we learn what may be expected in future."

The "Dead Sea" of America.

Flowing north from Utah Lake through part of the Great Basin, and emptying into the Great Salt Lake, the Dead Sea of America, is the river Jordan. Utah Lake is fresh water and abounds in fish; Salt Lake, as its name suggests, is so briny that no fish can live in its waters. To President Brigham Young and the worthy band of Pioneers, the Salt Lake Valley with the "Dead Sea" reflecting the glorious rays of a July sun, was indeed a "promised land."

The "Dead Sea" of the Holy Land.

Away across the Atlantic Ocean, stretching along the east shore of the Mediterranean Sea is another salt sea, another river Jordan, and another fresh water lake, and the river flows through the "Promised Land," or the Land of Canaan. However, if you will refer to a map of that country, you will see that the relative position of this lake, river and sea are just opposite in direction from these in Utah. In the Holy Land the fresh water lake is in the north, and the Jordan river flows south into the Dead Sea.

The land that contains these three important marks in history has several names. As given above, it is called The Holy Land; also The Land of Canaan; also the Land of the Hebrews, or the Land of Israel, because Jacob's children once settled there; also the Land of Judah, after one of Jacob's sons; also Palestine, probably after the Philistines, who lived, as you know, in the days of the shepherd boy David.

Size of Cannan.

Salt Lake is eighty miles long and about forty miles wide. The Land of Canaan is about twice as long and twice as wide; or in extreme length about one hundred seventy miles, and its width about eighty. The City of Dan was in the northern part, and Beersheba in the southern part; so when you hear the expression "from Dan to Beersheba," you will know that it once denoted the entire length of the land of Canaan.

Sea of Galilee.

The fresh water lake, of the Holy Land, also has several names. It is known generally as the "Sea of Galilee;" but it is also called "Sea of Tiberias," "Lake of Gennesareth," "Lake of Tiberias," and the "Sea of Cenneroth." It is about sixteen miles long and six miles wide. "The waters of this lake lie in a deep basin, surrounded on all sides with lofty hills, excepting only the narrow entrance and outlet of the Jordan at each extreme. * * * The appearance of this sea from the town of Capernaum, which is situated near the upper end of the bank on the western side, is extremely grand; its greatest length runs nearly north and south. The barren aspect of the mountains on each side, and the total absence of wood give, however, a cast of dullness to the picture, which is increased to melancholy by the dead calm of its waters."

On the west side of this lake was one of the important divisions of Palestine, called Galilee. One ancient writer says that at one time this province "contained two hundred and four cities and towns, the least of which contained fifteen thousand inhabitants."[1]

Bethsaida.

Somewhere in this province, probably very near Capernaum, was a little town called Bethsaida. There was another town by this name on the north-eastern shore, but it is the Bethsaida, near Capernaum, in which we are now most interested. To must have been near the lake, because many of the men who lived there made their living by fishing, not with poles and hooks and lines, as the boys fish for trout in our mountain streams, but with nets, which they let down from their boats, and with which they dragged the lake until they would entangle the fish, which they then hauled to shore.

Simon.

In one of these fishermen's homes, probably a few years before the Savior's birth, was born one day, a little baby boy whom his parents named Simon or Simeon. He had a brother named Andrew.[2] Their father's name was Jonas or Johanna, but very little is known about him, and nothing about their mother.

Simon's Home and Boyhood.

Nothing definite is known about either Simon's childhood or his boyhood. However, we are safe to conclude from what we know about the customs, beliefs, and practices of the Jews of his time that

[1] Josephus
[2] John 1:42-43

he lived in a small, flat-roofed house containing very little, if any, furniture; that either at home or at school, perhaps at both, he learned all about the prophets in what is now our Old Testament; that he observed the Sabbath day strictly; and what is most important of all, he learned to look forward to the day when the Savior of the world would come to His people.

In fancy, we can picture Simon and Andrew and their playmates amusing themselves on the shore of Galilee; but it is only in imagination that we can see any of the incidents in Simon's childhood. "We may think of him," writes George L. Weed, "as a useful boy, helping his mother in the labors of the house—carefully bringing the little red clay lamps for trimming, or the corn to be parched, or the fish his father had caught, or the charcoal on which it was to be cooked, or the bread from the oven, and the oil and honey-cakes to be eaten with it, or water from the stream that flowed from the hill behind their home into the lake, or filling the water-jars at the door. Was he not his mother's joy when for the first time he shook the olives from the trees and brought them to her as a part of their frugal meal; or when he spread the maize and hemp to dry on the flat roof in the summer sun? Was he not his father's pride the first time he handled the oar, and dipped it aright in the wave, and helped to spread the net, and counted the fish they had caught? He watched the flight of the sparrows and gathered the flowers—poppies, daisies and anemones—like those from which the Great Teacher, whom now he knew not, would teach him lessons of wisdom and love. Childlike, he gathered shells upon the seashore, and dug in the white sand of the beach with a rude stick, with delight equal to that of the boy of today with his finished toy-shovel and little painted pail."

None of the fishermen who saw Simon with his playmates scampering around the nets and boats ever suspected that he would grow up to be among the greatest men of the world!

Some writers tell us that the Galileans were generally brave and fearless, and loved liberty. The men made good soldiers for they were "bold and intrepid." The boy, Simon, as he grew to manhood must have admired the brave, bold men around him, for he, too, became a man of strong character, as we learn from the first recorded instance of his life.

SIMON'S NAME CHANGED

Simon Hears John the Baptist.

Soon after Simon had grown to manhood there came a man from the wilderness of Jordan, clothed only in camel's hair and a leathern girdle about his loins, but preaching with such mighty power that people from "Judea and all the regions round about" came to hear him. This great preacher was John the Baptist, the forerunner of Christ. Among those who came to hear him was Simon, who, no doubt, rejoiced to hear this preacher of Repentance declare that the Son of Man was about to come to the earth. Simon, Andrew and some of their friends believed what the Baptist taught.

One day, when, with some of his followers, John was near Bethabara (a word which means "a place of crossing") he saw Jesus coming toward them, and said:

"Behold the Lamb of God."

"Behold the Lamb of God, who taketh away the sin of the world! This is He of whom I said, After me cometh a man who is preferred before me." Again, the next day, probably about 10 o'clock in the morning, John was standing talking with two of his disciples. They were Andrew, Simon's brother, and John. Walking a short distance from them was the same man whom John had pointed out the day before as the Lamb of God "And looking upon Jesus as He walked, John saith, Behold the Lamb of God. And the two disciples heard him speak, and they followed Jesus."

Simon's Brother Believes in Jesus.

Accepting the invitation of Jesus to go with Him to the place where He stayed, these two men remained with Him, listening to His words all the rest of the day. When they left, they believed that Jesus was the King of Israel, the Savior of the world. Thus they became, in that day the first two, beside John the Baptist, to believe in Jesus.

Whenever we have anything which is really good, we always desire to share it with one we love. It was so with these two brothers. They no sooner felt the divine influence that radiated from the Savior than they were filled with a desire to bring those whom they loved under that same influence. Andrew went out to find his brother Simon, and John to find his brother James. Andrew found Simon first, and said:

"We have found the Messiah, which is, being interpreted, the Christ."

Simon is Called "Cephas."

And he brought him to Jesus, and when Jesus beheld him, He said, "Thou are Simon the son of Jonas: thou shalt be called Cephas, which is by interpretation, A stone" (or The Rock).

In those days the Jews spoke the Hebrew language; but the new Testament was written in the Greek language. Now, in Hebrew

"Cephas" means "rock;" but in Greek the word for "rock" is "Petras," or "Peter." So from that time, Simon was known as Simon Peter, or "Simon, the Rock."

When we think of this wonderful world in which we live, of its great division of land called continents; that in the eastern continent there are the countries of Europe, Asia, and Africa; that in one little corner of Asia, there is a strip of land only about twice as long and twice as wide as our Salt Lake; that in that strip of land was a division, like one of our counties, called Galilee; that in this province were over two hundred cities, and in each city several thousand people, among whom one day was born a little baby whose parents were unknown; that this baby boy grew to be a man of such strong character that Jesus named him "a Rock," and for nineteen hundred years now he has been known and honored by millions and millions of people—when we think of all these things we must surely realize, even in our youth, that a humble birth is no hindrance to greatness.

"CHRIST AND JOHN."

LESSON 3 A Period of Preparation

"Oh, be my friend, and teach me to be thine."

"Great souls by instinct to each other turn,
Demand alliance, and in friendship burn."

Home in Capernaum

Peter's Views of the Messiah.

From the moment Peter met Jesus, his views of life were changed. Up to that time, he had looked for the coming of the King of the Jews as an event the indefinite future. With other Jews, he had anticipated that the Savior's coming would be marked by wonderful manifestations, and that, clad in purple robes, and attended by many angels. He would come in mighty power, and in one divine expression of His wrath, strike the Roman shackles from the conquered Jewish nation.

But now, Peter had met the Messiah—a lone man on the banks of the Jordan! Only about five men knew of His claim to the Messiahship. There were no legions of heavenly hosts accompanying Him! He wore no purple robes! He possessed no visible means at hand with which to break the Roman yoke! Was He, indeed, the Messiah that was to come, or should Peter look for another?

Jesus' Influence Over Peter.

These and a hundred other thoughts, undoubtedly crowded Peter's mind, as he left the wilderness of Jordan to return to his fishing in Galilee. Andrew and John, on that memorable visit, seemed to have received a testimony of the divinity of Jesus' mission, and they bore that testimony to their brothers when they so joyously exclaimed, "We have found the Messiah!" But Peter—impetuous Peter, who, we shall learn, was naturally outspoken, had not yet so far as we know, expressed such assurance. However, he was deeply impressed; for had not Jesus, at first sight, read his character? Had He not penetrated into his inmost nature? and had He not radiated a spirit that so completely enveloped Peter that from its influence the fisherman never more desired to go?

Peter's Home.

Peter at this time was a married man, and was perhaps the father of a little boy. He had moved from his old home in Bethsaida, and lived with his wife's mother, or she with him, in Capernaum. With him were also Andrew and their two faithful companions and friends, James and John, the sons of Zebedee.

Peter's home became the most distinguished home in all Capernaum, and later one of the most memorable spots in all the world. Here, undoubtedly, Jesus stayed whenever He was at Capernaum! Indeed after Jesus had been so ruthlessly rejected by His own townsmen in Nazareth, He made Capernaum His "own city;" and it is supposed that much of the time, the honor fell upon Peter to entertain in his home the Savior of the world. How every word, every act on the part of his worthy guest must surely have increased Peter's confidence in Jesus as the Messiah!

A Lesson in Obedience

On Shores of Galilee.

One beautiful morning, several months after the events narrated in the previous lesson, and a short time following His rejection from Nazareth, Jesus was preaching to a multitude on the shores of Galilee. Peter and Andrew were busy near-by washing their nets, after having spent all night on the lake in a futile attempt to catch some fish.

"And it came to pass, that, as the people pressed upon Jesus to hear the word of God, He stood by the lake of Gennesaret,

"And saw two ships standing by the lake: but the fishermen were gone out of them, and were washing their nets.

"And He entered into one of the ships, which was Simon's, and prayed him that he would thrust out a little from the land. And He sat down, and taught the people out of the ship."[3]

First Recorded Instance of Peter's Obedience.

When Peter complied with Jesus' request "to thrust out a little from the land," he performed the first recorded instance of his obedience to Christ's word. Now, however, followed a command obedience to which was directly contrary to the fisherman's judgment. When Jesus had finished speaking to the people, He said to Peter,

"Launch out into the deep, and let down your nets for toiled all the night, and have taken nothing." As much as from the empty net; it was dry, and the broken threads mended. Peter was tired and wanted rest. He was hungry, too, and perhaps discouraged. No wonder, then, that Peter answered and said, "Master, we have toiled all night, and have taken nothing." As much as to say, "What is the use? There are no fish this morning in this part of the lake, nor has there been all

---

[3] Luke 5:1-3

night!" But Peter was learning to honor and obey this Man among men; so he quickly added these words: "Nevertheless at Thy word, I will let down the net."[4]

As an experienced fisherman, his *judgment* said to make a further attempt was useless; as a follower of Jesus, his *Faith* bade him try.

Result of Obedience.

"And when they had this done, they enclosed a great multitude of fishes: and their net brake. And they beckoned unto their partners which were in the other ship, that they should come and help them. And they came, and filled both ships so that they began to sink."

We are told that Peter "was astonished, and all that were with him, at the draught of the fishes which they had taken." Peter, the leader of the four as he was afterwards the head of the Twelve, "fell down at Jesus' knees, saying. Depart from me: for I am a sinful man, O Lord."[5]

Was it just the doubt and hesitancy expressed when, a few minutes before, Jesus had asked him to "push cut into the deep," or was it the realization of many such doubts of Christ's divinity that now overwhelmed him, and made him sense his own inferiority and weakness in the presence of this Mighty One? Jesus had manifested His power, and in so doing had taught Peter the lesson that he and all the world, sooner or later, must learn; viz., that obedience to Christ's words brings blessings, temporal as well as spiritual. As the realization of this truth was pouring balm on his awe-struck feelings, Jesus said unto him, "*Fear not; from henceforth thou shalt catch men.*"[6]

A MEMORABLE SABBATH.[7]

After Jesus had been rejected from His own city, Nazareth, He "came down to Capernaum, and taught them on the Sabbath days."

Service in Synagogue.

The last part of a service in the synagogue in those days was the expounding of the scriptures, and preaching from them to the people. This was done not always by an officer but by some distinguished person who might be in the congregation. Of course, Jesus was known all around by this time as a great teacher, a worker of miracles,

---

[4] Luke 5:5
[5] Luke 5:8
[6] Luke 5:10
[7] Luke 4:31-40

and an able interpreter of the law; and, "they were astonished at His doctrine: for His word was with power."

An Evil Spirit Rebuked.

On one particular Sabbath, when Jesus was preaching, Peter and all present were surprised to see a man rise in the audience, and suddenly interrupt by crying out in a loud voice,

"Let us alone; what have we to do with Thee, Thou Jesus of Nazareth? Art Thou come to destroy us? I know Thee who Thou art; the Holy One of God." As this man, who was possessed of an evil spirit, ceased his railing, each person in the congregation must have almost held his breath, as Jesus rebuked the evil one by saying,

"Hold thy peace and come out of him. And when the devil had thrown him in the midst, he came out of him, and hurt him not.

"And they were all amazed, and spake among themselves saying, What a word is this! for with authority and power, He commandeth the unclean spirits and they come out."[8]

At the conclusion of this service, Jesus went with Peter to the latter's home, Andrew, and James and John accompanying them. Peter, Andrew, James and John—these four who were playmates in boyhood, partners as fishermen, companions as disciples of John the Baptist, are now becoming inseparable in the loving bonds of the Brotherhood of Christ! As they entered the house, they learned that Simon's wife's mother was very sick of fever. Undoubtedly, it was Peter who told Jesus of his mother-in-law's condition, and pleaded, either by word or look, or both, that He would bless her. Jesus "took her by the hand and lifted her up; and immediately the fever left her, and she ministered unto them."

You can imagine that all Capernaum was talking about how Jesus had rebuked the evil spirit from the afflicted man in the synagogue! And then, a few minutes after the service, He healed a woman instantly of a fever! The news spread from house to house, and from group to group until "the fame of Him went out into every place of the country round about."

Many Healed.

All that afternoon, Peter's house and the streets around it were packed with crowds of people, some out of curiosity but most of them desiring a blessing. Men possessed of devils were taken through the crowd to Jesus and were cured; those who had been suffering for days of a burning fever, those who were afflicted with various kinds of

---

[8] Luke 4:36

diseases, were all brought into the presence of this Great Physician, who "laid His hands on everyone of them, and healed them."

Through the Twilight and Evening.

The sun went down, twilight came, and evening shades began to deepen into night, but still the sick and suffering sought that divine healing which only Christ the Lord could give. "Never," says Eidersheim, "Never, surely, was He more truly the Christ than when, in the stillness of that evening, He went through that suffering throng laying His hands in the blessing of healing upon every one of them and casting out many devils."

It was probably late that night before Jesus could go to His rest. Even later, after the people had gone to their now happier homes, Peter and his household would desire to talk to their honored guest about the wonderful miracles of that day. At length, however, all retired, and everybody in the house slept as the midnight hours of that never-to-be-forgotten Sabbath passed into the early morning hours of Sunday.

Another Week of Preparation

Sunday Morning.

Before daylight came, however, Jesus arose quietly, and walked out into the morning air, sought a quiet, "solitary" place, and there prayed.

"His pure thoughts were borne
Like fumes of sacred incense o'er the clouds,
And wafted them on angels' wings, to ways
Of light, to the bright source of all."

Peter must have been surprised when upon going to greet Jesus with a bright "Good-morning," he found the guest-chamber empty. Perhaps he guessed where Jesus had gone; for we are told that, "Simon and they that were with him followed after Him. And when they had found Him, they said unto Him,

"*All men seek Thee*!"

What a glorious condition will be in this old world when it can be truthfully said to Christ,

"*All men seek Thee*!"

"All Men Seek Thee."

Selfishness, envy, hatred, lying, stealing, cheating, disobedience to parents, cruelty to children and to dumb animals, quarreling among neighbors, and fighting among nations—all will be no more when it can be truthfully said to the Redeemer of mankind,

"All men seek Thee!"

Around Galilee.

It seems that Jesus and His friends left Capernaum that day, and "Preached in synagogues throughout all Gililee, and cast out devils." Wherever they went the sick were healed, and the lepers were cleansed. Some days afterwards, they returned to Capernaum. No sooner did the people learn that Jesus was in "the house" (undoubtedly Peter's house) than "Straightway many were gathered together, insomuch that there was no room to receive them, no, not so much as about the door: and He preached the word unto them."

A Man Sick of Palsy.

It was on this occasion that four men brought a man sick of palsy. The poor man lay on his bed, each corner of which was held by one of the four men. Finding it impossible because of the crowd to gain entrance to the house by the door, they went on the roof. Here they made an opening into the room below, "And let down the bed wherein the sick of the palsy lay."

"When Jesus saw their faith, He said unto the sick of palsy, Son, thy sins be forgiven thee.

"And immediately he arose, took up the bed, and went forth before them all; insomuch that they were all amazed, and glorified God, saying: We never saw it on this fashion." All these glorious manifestations of divine power, and, undoubtedly, many, many more, Jesus had given even before He chose His Twelve Apostles.

Peter's Faith Strengthened.

Peter, as you see, was a witness of them all. If he had had any doubts a few months previous, when his brother Andrew said, "We have found the Messiah," surely they had long since been banished from his mind; and we can readily understand why, when Jesus said, "Henceforth thou shalt catch men," Peter "forsook all and followed Him."

But even yet, notwithstanding all his experiences, Simon's faith is not the Rock that Jesus would have it become.

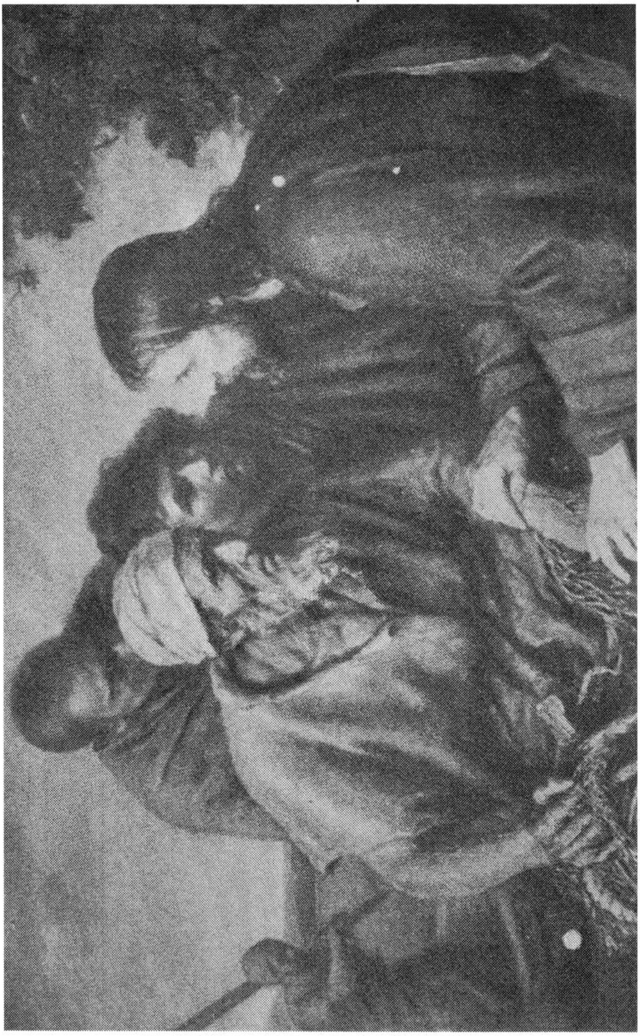

CHRIST AND THE FISHERMEN.
"From henceforth thou shalt catch men."

LESSON 4 A Special Witness

"The Twelve traveling counselors are called to be the Twelve Apostles, or special witnesses of the name of Christ in all the world."

A Night of Prayer.

Probably several months after the events narrated in the previous chapter and a little while before the Feast of the Passover, Jesus went out to a mountain near Capernaum. As was usual, now, in His life, a large crowd followed Him. But He left the crowd, and went to the top of the mountain, so he could be all alone with His Father in Heaven, unto whom He prayed all night.

Twelve Chosen.

Undoubtedly, many of his most ardent followers remained at the mountain also all night, for "When it was day, He called unto Him His disciples, and of them He chose twelve, whom also He named apostles."[9]

The word Apostle means an "Envoy" or "one who is sent." An apostle is a "Special witness of the name of Christ in all the world."

In all the accounts given of this important event, Peter's name is mentioned first, indicating that he was chosen as the chief apostle, and was undoubtedly appointed and set apart as the President of the Council of Twelve. The names of the Twelve whom Jesus ordained at that time were:

(1) Simon Peter, and his brother (2) Andrew; (3) James and (4) John, the two sons of Zebedee; (5) Philip of Bethsaida, and (6) Nathanael, also called Bartholomew; (7) Thomas, also called "Didymus," a name which means "a twin;" (8) Matthew, the publican, or tax gatherer; (9) James, the son of Alphaeus, called "James the Less;" (10) Lebbeus, who was also called Thaddeus, and also Judas, but not Judas Iscariot; (11) Simon, the "Canaanite," or "Simon the Zelotes," and (12) Judas Iscariot, who became the traitor.

---

[9] Luke 6:13

ST. MATTHEW.

Who the Twelve Were.

These twelve men were, for the most part, Galilean fishermen who labored at their trade on the shores of Galilee. Matthew, however, was a publican, and therefore despised by the Jews; and Judas was a Judean. Some of the leaders of the Jews thought that they were "unlearned and ignorant men.[10] Unlearned they were; but not ignorant; for by their wisdom and preaching, they overthrew the

[10] Acts 4:13

whole edifice of human wisdom, and led the world to the light of truth."

As a humble disciple of Jesus, Peter had been a "witness" of many wonderful things pertaining to the Savior's mission; but it was difficult for him to comprehend the significance of the Gospel plan. You will note as we proceed with his biography that his understanding of it unfolded slowly, even though he was almost constantly, for the next year or so, in the presence of his Lord. Here are some of the things which he witnessed immediately after his ordination to the Apostleship.

AT MATTHEW'S FEAST

One day Jesus and the Twelve accepted an invitation to Matthew's house, a circumstance that made the Pharisees much offended because Jesus ate "with publicans and the sinners. While Jesus and the Twelve were still at the feast, and Jesus was answering the charge of the Pharisees,

Jairus

"Behold, there cometh one of the rulers of the Synagogue, Jairus, by name; and when he saw him, he fell at his feet, and besought him greatly saying,

"My little daughter lieth at the point of death; I pray thee, come and lay thy hands on her, that she may be healed, and she shall live."[11]

Jesus immediately left the pleasures of the feast and of the entertainment of his friend and brother, Matthew, and followed Jairus to the latter's house.

THE AFFLICTED WOMAN

Faith of an Afflicted Woman.

"And much people followed him, and thronged him."[12] In this crowd was a woman who had been suffering for twelve years from a sore that could not be healed. The blood had wasted for so long a time that she was weak, and she was very poor, for "she had spent all she had" trying to get cured. She had heard of Jesus and of His power to heal the sick, and she had such faith that she said to herself, "If I may touch but his clothes, I shall be made whole."

As Jesus passed, she stretched forth her hand and touched just the hem of his garment, "and straightway the fountain of her blood was dried up; and she felt in her body that she was healed of that plague."

"Who Touched My Clothes?"

[11] Mark 5:22-23

[12] Mark 5:24

Jesus, too, immediately feeling that "Virtue" had gone out of him, turned and asked, "Who touched my clothes?" Peter answered, "Master, the multitude throng and press thee and sayest thou. Who touched me?"[13]

What an insight must Peter have received into Christ's divine powers and susceptibility as he noted the afflicted woman come through the crowd and throw herself at the feet of Jesus, confessing all before him! What satisfaction must have been his, as he heard his Lord say, "Daughter, thy faith hath made thee whole; go in peace, and be whole of thy plague."[14] But Peter was soon to witness even a greater miracle.

JAIRUS' LITTLE DAUGHTER

Jairus' Daughter Dead.

While Jesus was yet speaking to the now blessed and happy woman, and while Peter and his fellow councilmen and the multitude gazed in wonder, "there cometh one from the ruler of the Synagogue's house, saying to him, 'Thy daughter is dead; trouble not the Master.'"

Poor Jairus! He had hurried from the bedside of his little girl only a half hour or so ago to plead with Jesus of Nazareth to come and save his little daughter. The Divine Physician had started immediately, but it was too late. The great destroyer, Death, had claimed the little girl. Peter's heart must have ached in sympathy for the sorrowing father. But, listen! Following the gloomy announcement of death, they hear the comforting voice of Jesus: "Fear not; believe only, and she shall be made whole."

Jairus' Daughter Restored.

As they neared the house, they heard the weeping of friends and the moans of the broken-hearted mother. But Peter, and others, too, heard the Master say, "Weep not; she is not dead, but sleepeth. And they laughed Him to scorn, knowing that she was dead."[15] The Savior then told everybody to leave the room excepting Peter, James, and John, the father and the mother. He then walked up to the bed, took the little cold white hand in his, and said,

"Maid, arise.

"And her spirit came again, and she arose straightway: and he commanded to give her meat."

These incidents in the life of Peter are only a few of the glorious experiences he witnessed even before he went out as "a special witness of the name of Christ." Jesus knew that neither Peter nor

---

[13] Luke 8:45
[14] Mark 5:34
[15] Luke 8:52, 53

anybody else could convert others to the truth until he himself first knew that truth. No one can teach others what he himself does not know. Undoubtedly by this time Peter believed, with all his heart, that Jesus the Worker of Wonders, was indeed the Messiah who should come; but his testimony was not yet firm as a *rock.*

PETER'S FIRST MISSION

However, the time had come when he was sufficiently instructed to be able to go on a mission, "And Jesus called unto Him the Twelve, and began to send them forth by two and two;"[16]

Peter's Commission.

"And commanded them saying, Go not into the way of the Gentiles, and into any city of the Samaritans enter ye not: But go rather to the lost sheep of the house of Israel, and as ye go preach, saying, The kingdom of heaven is at hand Heal the sick, cleanse the lepers, raise the dead, cast out devils; freely ye have received, freely give."[17]

He told them to travel without money and without extra coats, and to carry blessings and peace to all who would receive them. He told them they would be persecuted, arrested and tried before governors and kings; but He assured them that the Lord would deliver them.

He further said that, "Whosoever shall not receive you, nor hear your words, when ye depart out of that house or city, shake off the dust of your feet. Verily I say unto you. It shall be more tolerable for the land of Sodom and Gomorra in the day of judgment than for that city."

"He that receiveth you receiveth me, and he that receiveth me receiveth Him that sent me. And whosoever shall give to drink unto one of these little ones a cup of cold water only in the name of a disciple, verily I say unto you, he shall in no wise lose his reward."

We do not know who Peter's companion was on this mission; but we are told that they went and preached that men should repent; that they cast out many devils, anointed with oil, and healed the sick, and did many other wonderful things in the name of Jesus of Nazareth.

John the Baptist Beheaded.

While they were on this mission, John Baptist the Baptist was beheaded by order of the wicked king Herod.

---

[16] Mark 6

[17] Matt. 10:5-42

In a Desert Place Opposite Capernaum.

Upon their return unto Jesus, "The Apostles gathered themselves together (probably at Capernaum) and told Him all things, both what they had done, and what they had taught." But there were so many people "coming and going" that "they had no leisure so much as to eat;" so Jesus desiring to be alone with the Twelve said, "Come ye yourselves apart into a desert place, and rest awhile." So they entered a ship privately and sailed from the Capernaum side to the northwest coast. But some of the people saw them departing and ran on foot around the northern coast of the lake. Other people saw these running, and joined them so that when Jesus and the Twelve landed, there were hundreds if not thousands of people there to greet them.

As evening approached, the disciples asked Jesus to send the multitude away, so they could go to their cities and buy something to eat.

Another Manifestation.

It was on this occasion that Peter witnessed another manifestation of the power of God, and had repeated the valuable lesson he learned over a year before, when he made a miraculous draught of fishes; viz., That obedience to Christ's words always brings comfort and happiness. Instead of sending the multitude away hungry, Jesus said, "Whence shall we buy bread that these might eat?"

The Multitude Fed.

Philip answered, "Two hundred pennyworth of bread is not sufficient for them, that every one of them may take a little." But from five barley loaves and two small fishes, Jesus, by some process natural to Him but miraculous to us, fed that vast crowd of people, numbering about five thousand.

Peter assisted not only in distributing the bread and fish among the companies, but also in gathering the twelve baskets full left. No doubt he was one of those who said, "This is of a truth that Prophet that should come into the world." Let us hope, however, that he was not one of those who would have taken Jesus by force to make Him king.

LESSON 5 Peter's Faith Tested

"The steps of faith fall on the seeming void, but find the rock beneath."
"All I have seen teaches me to trust the Creator for all I have not seen."

Genuine Faith.

When Jesus called Simon "Peter" or "The Rock," he undoubtedly expressed in that name one characteristic which He desired to see in the faith of His disciples, and particularly in each of His Apostles. He desired them to possess a faith that was unwavering,—a faith that would make them steadfast in the truth regardless of miracles or the acts of men—a faith that would trust the Lord at all times and under all circumstances, let those times and circumstances be what they may. Jesus knew that the Jews were easily influenced; that a miracle performed today might awaken a feeling in them that He was the King for whom they had been waiting, and that a truth taught tomorrow might arouse in them a feeling that He was an impostor. He wanted to lead them to God and to His Gospel. He longed to have them comprehend the truths of life so they would live them after He was gone from their midst.

Jesus Grieved.

Imagine, then, how grieved He must have been when, after the miracle mentioned in the last chapter, the people arose and hailed Him King and thought by offering Him the bauble of an empty crown, they were doing Him honor! He did not want them to honor Him. His desire was for them to see the power of God, and believe in His divine truth.

Desiring to be alone once more with His Father, not wanting the company even of the three chief apostles, Peter, James, and John, Jesus dismissed the multitude, told the Twelve to get into the ship and sail back to Capernaum, and He retired to a solitary place to pray.

A TEMPESTUOUS SEA

A Storm.

During the night, while Jesus was yet praying, a great storm arose, which stirred the lake into a seething mass of billows. From the mountain Jesus could see His disciples battling with the sea, but unable to make much headway, although they could not see Him.

When the ship was about thirty furlongs (four miles) from the shore, Jesus decided to go into it. It was now past midnight, and the disciples were still struggling in the midst of the heaving sea.

Jesus on the Water.

Imagine their fear when through the darkness they saw an object coming towards them on the waves! And when someone cried out, "It's a Spirit!" they were more frightened than ever.

"But straightway Jesus spoke unto them, saying. Be of good cheer; It is I; be not afraid."

At once, Peter spoke out, saying, "Lord, if it be Thou, bid me come unto Thee on the water."[18]

Peter's Faith.

"Come," said Jesus.

"And when Peter was come down out of the ship, he walked on the water, to go to Jesus."

Peter, firm in belief and strong in determination, when your eye sees only the majesty of faith and the perfect manifestation of its power! Mighty and fearless when your eye sees only the glory of God, and your soul cries out to go to Him!

His Doubt.

But when you see "the wind boisterous," you are afraid; and beginning to sink, cry, saying, "Lord, save me."

So it is in life: when the winds of temptation and the waves of despair beat upon us, the eye of faith is turned more upon these raging elements than upon the Light of Life, the power of faith is thus weakened, and as Peter, we begin to sink. Too many, ah, too many go down beneath the billows; only a few cry out as he. "Lord, save us!"

And immediately Jesus stretched forth His hand, and caught him, and said unto him, "O, thou of little faith, wherefore didst thou doubt?"

ANOTHER TEST

In Capernaum.

Next morning, the people in Capernaum who knew that Peter and the other disciples had left the opposite shore without Jesus, were very much astonished to see Him in their midst, and said, Rabbi, when camest thou hither?

"Ye seek me," answered Jesus, "not because ye saw the miracles, but because ye did eat of the loaves, and were filled."

---

[18] Matt. 14:28

"Lord, save me."

"Labor not for the meat which perisheth, but for that meat which endureth unto everlasting life, which the Son of Man shall give unto you."[19]

Sermon on the Bread of Life.

He then delivered the famous sermon on the Bread of Life, part of which, as John remembered it, is recorded in John the sixth chapter. There were so many things spoken which the Jews could not understand, because of their prejudice, that they first became confused, then angry, and finally much offended. Those who had only

[19] John 6:25-27

a little faith, became influenced by the murmuring crowd, and said, "We don't believe this man is the Son of God." Even some of His disciples turned away from the Truth, and "walked no more with Him."

Men Swerved by Doubt.

The mass of angry men and women became much like the heaving sea that tossed the disciples the evening before. The winds of ridicule and the waves of discontent beat against the wavering disciples. As they looked upon these angry elements of human passion, their faith in Christ weakened, and they "began to sink."

Jesus Appeals to the Twelve.

In vain, Jesus testified, "It is I, the Son of man!" They would not listen to Him, for He was to them only the son of Joseph the carpenter. As group after group turned their backs upon Him. He turned to the Twelve and said, "Will ye also go away?"

Peter's Answer.

Again it was Peter who broke the silence. With the others, he had looked at the noisy crowd, with the others he had listened to the angry words hurled at their Master. In the midst of this sea of human passion, shall he say, "Lord, if it be Thee, bid me come unto Thee?"

As if he wavered just a little, as if his faith had not yet become as firm as Jesus would have it become, he answered, "Lord, to whom shall we go? Thou hast the words of eternal life."

Belief Matures into Knowledge.

Then, as his assurance became stronger and his thoughts turned from the apostate crowd, he added, "And we *believe*—and are *sure* that thou are the Christ, the Son of the living God." Though there came not from Jesus' lips at this time, the word "Blessed," yet, undoubtedly, He was gratified indeed to see the wavering faith of His disciples become steadfast in the heart of His Apostles, as if they would say,

"Then come the wild weather, come sleet or come snow,
We will stand by each other, however it blow.
Oppression and sickness, and sorrow, and pain
Shall be to our true love as links in a chain."

LESSON 6 Peter's Testimony

At Tyre and Sidon.

Very soon after the people of Capernaum rejected the Savior, as narrated in the previous chapter, Jesus took His Twelve disciples westward across Galilee into the land of Tyre and Sidon, near the Mediterranean Sea. He desired to be alone with the Twelve that He might teach them many things pertaining to the kingdom of God, and thus prepare them for carrying on the work, after He should leave them.

There were many things happened on this tour which must have made it a memorable one to Peter and the other members of the Twelve. First, there was the Gentile woman who sought Jesus, and implored Him to come and heal her little daughter.

A Syro-Phoenician Woman.

Because she did not belong to the Jewish race, the disciples said: "Master, send this woman away, for she is a trouble to us, crying out after us." Of course, they thought then, and a long time afterwards, that the Gospel was only for the Jews. But Jesus taught them that He loved the Gentile woman just as well as He did the Jews. But Peter did not fully understand.

Other Miracles.

From the coast of Tyre and Sidon, they traveled around Galilee and came to the east side of the Sea of Galilee. Here the disciples witnessed further manifestations of the power of Jesus. A deaf man who could not speak plainly was made to hear and to speak; and when the people heard about it, they followed Jesus and the Twelve out of the village into "a desert place."

Again Peter saw a multitude of people fed; this time from only seven loaves and a few small fishes.

It would seem that after all these months with the Savior—hearing His parables, seeing His miracles, feeling His spirit and receiving His teachings daily, the apostles would surely understand the mission of the Redeemer.

Jesus' Sayings Not Understood.

But we read that after these "four thousand men besides women and children" were fed, the disciples entered with Jesus into a boat and rowed across to the west side of the lake. Here they met some

Pharisees and Sadducees who began to oppose Jesus. When He and the Twelve were alone again, He said: "Take heed and beware of the leaven of the Pharisees and of the Sadducees."

You know what Jesus meant when He said this; but the disciples said to themselves, "He says this 'because we have brought no bread.'"

When Jesus saw that they did not comprehend Him, He said: "How is it that ye do not understand that I spake it not to you concerning bread, that ye should beware of the leaven of the Pharisees and of the Sadducees?"

"Then understood they how that He bade them not beware of the leaven of bread, but of the doctrine of the Pharisees and of the Sadducees."[20]

Undoubtedly, there were several among them whose testimony was becoming firm and unwavering. At any rate, we learn that just a few days later, the chief apostle gave evidence in words that could not be misunderstood, of his sure conviction that Christ was indeed the Son of the Living God.

Peter's Memorable Testimony.

They had gone northward to Caesarea Philippi at the foot of Mount Hermon. Here, Jesus, one day, asked His disciples this question: "Who do men say that I, the Son of man, am?"

They answered, "Some say thou art John the Baptist. Some say thou art Elias, and others, Jeremias, or one of the prophets."

Then Jesus said, "But who say ye that I am?"

Simon Peter answered,

"*Thou art the Christ, the Son of the Living God.*"

There is no hesitancy now, no fear, no wavering, no "we believe and are sure;" but the unqualified and direct expression of a soul convinced of the truth: "Thou art the Christ, the Son of the Living God."

"*Blessed* art thou, Simon Barjona," said Jesus, "for flesh and blood hath not revealed this unto thee, but my Father which is in heaven."[21]

At last Jesus discovers the assurance in Peter for which He has been laboring many months to develop. He now knows that Peter's spirit has received divine assurance that all these miracles and mighty manifestations have been wrought by the power of God through His only Begotten Son. He knows that the testimony borne by Peter

[20] Matt. 16:1-12

[21] Matt. 16:13-20

comes not from men but from God, and no matter what men may think or do, Peter will stand firm as a rock on this testimony.

"I say unto thee," continued Jesus, "that thou art Peter, and upon this rock will I build my church; and the gates of hell shall not prevail against it."

Christ's Church Built Upon Revelation.

By that He meant that as Simon's name "Peter" means rock, so this testimony that comes by revelation shall be the rock upon which Christ's Church Christ's shall be built. Because when one receives such divine assurance in his soul that the gospel is true, no views of men, nor waves of temptation nor "the power of hell" can deprive him of it. You remember when Jesus first met Simon, He said He should be called "the Rock." Ever since then it would seem that Jesus has been waiting for the time when Peter's testimony would be like his character—expressive and firm. That time has come; and Peter is now prepared to receive a greater responsibility.

Keys of the Kingdom

"And I will give unto thee the keys of the kingdom of heaven; and whatsoever thou shall bind on earth shall be bound in heaven; and whatsoever thou shalt loose on earth shall be loosed in heaven."

One key was to open the door of the gospel to the Gentiles, but it took quite a while before Peter knew how to use it.

It is one thing to know that the gospel is true; it is quite another thing to comprehend its purpose and significance.

Jesus Foretells His Death.

From that time, Jesus began to tell the Apostles that He would suffer and die, and that they must carry on the preaching of the gospel. He told them Jesus that in a few months He would be taken by the chief priests, would be killed, and would rise again the third day.

Misguided Zeal.

When Peter heard this, he took the Savior off to one side, and still hoping that Jesus would some day be a king, said, "Far be it from Thee, Lord; this shall not be unto Thee." As much as to say, "They shall not take you if we can prevent it."

Rebuked Peter.

Brave but uncomprehending Peter! He does not realize that it is necessary for his Lord to die, before His mission of redemption is fulfilled. So he would, in his blinded love, prevent his Master from completing His work! The Savior perceiving this, turned and said unto Peter, "Get thee behind me, Satan: thou art an offense unto me; for thou savorest not the things that be of God, but those that be of men."[22]

This was a severe rebuke, and it must have impressed Peter deeply with the thought that his plan was not God's plan; and he no doubt realized that there was yet very much for him to learn before he could carry out the great responsibility that the Lord had this day conferred upon him. But in his zeal to save Jesus from death, he erred, though only in love; and we can fancy hearing one of the others saying, in effect, in commendation of Peter's anxiety,

> "If he be not one that truly loves you,
> That errs in ignorance, and not in cunning,
> I have no judgment in an honest man's face."

At any rate, we know that Jesus was pleased with Peter's testimony, and with his love, and would patiently wait the unfolding of his mind in the comprehension of the gospel plan.

---

[22] Matt. 16:16-23

LESSON 7 A Marvelous Manifestation

The Holy Mount.

In the region of Caesarea Philippi, where Peter gave his testimony and received a blessing and power from his Master, is a high mountain peak of the Lebanon range, known as Mt. Hermon. Peter called it the Holy Mount. When you learn of what took place there, you will agree that Peter gave it a good name.

One writer who has visited this region tells us that the "glittering splendor" of this peak, "towering like a giant above all other peaks of the Lebanon range, its head always covered with snow, is visible from every direction. It is in clear view as far south as the Dead Sea. It was probably the highest spot of earth on which our Lord ever stood, and from which He had His most extensive view. From it He looked down upon Galilee, where He had taught and wrought, where He had been received by the few and rejected by the many."[23]

Self-Denial Necessary.

Six days, (Luke says eight) had passed since Peter had borne his great testimony—six days, undoubtedly of important instruction to Peter and the other eleven. It was probably during that time that the Twelve learned that to be a true follower of Jesus, one must be able to deny one's self of many desires and appetites—one must learn to control feelings of anger, jealousy, and other passions. Said the Savior, "If any man will come after me, let him deny himself, and take up his cross, and follow me.

"For whosoever will save his life, shall lose it:

"And whosoever will lose his life for my sake shall find it.

"For what is a man profited, if he shall gain the whole world, and lose his own soul? or what shall a man give in exchange for his soul?"[24]

These and many other glorious truths, Peter undoubtedly heard during that memorable week at Caesarea Philippi.

But he was to see and hear things even more glorious.

Still perplexed over some of the sayings of Jesus, still wondering why it was necessary for their Lord to "suffer many things, and be rejected" and even put to death, Peter and James and John one night, accompanied Jesus up the side of Mt. Hermon. It appears from the brief accounts we have of this incident that they spent several hours in

---

[23] Weed.

[24] Matt. 16:24-26

solemn conversation, the apostles "asking Him many questions concerning His sayings."

The Transfiguration.

Twilight deepened into darkness, and the shades of night completely hid Mt. Hermon from the sleeping vales below. Perhaps the three leaders became drowsy; and as their Lord withdrew a little apart to pray, they may have fallen, for a moment or two, into a sleep—Luke tells us that they were "heavy with sleep." Be that as it may, we know that when their eyes were turned toward Jesus, "He was transfigured before them. And His raiment became shining, exceeding white as snow; so white as no fuller on earth can white them."

"And there appeared unto them Elias and Moses, and they were talking with Jesus."[25]

Death but a Change.

These heavenly personages talked, not *to* Jesus but *with* him, about His approaching death, and resurrection, one of the vital things in Christ's ministry which Peter could not comprehend. Surely after this glorious vision of two heavenly beings. Death would lose much if not all its terror for Peter, James, and John. They would know that even if wicked men did kill their Master, that He would still live and still be their Lord and Savior. Death, to them, after this, would be just a "departure." They would realize that "Death hath nothing terrible in it, but what life hath made so."

"It is Good to be Here."

Peter by inspiration had received assurances that Jesus was indeed the Christ; now he witnessed a visible sign of his testimony. Desiring to have a monument to this outward sign, something which other eyes beside his might behold, he cried, out of the impulsiveness of his heart, "Master, it is good for us to be here, and let us make three tabernacles; one for thee, and one for Moses, and one for Elias." But suddenly, as Moses and Elias "departed," a cloud overshadowed them and a voice came *out of the cloud* saying, "*This* is My beloved Son hear Him!"

Sources of Testimony.

Peter's testimony was, by this time, made strong and his faith proved:[26]

---

[25] Matt. 17:1-8; Mark 9:1-6

(1) By the confirmation of miracles; (2) By seeing heavenly beings; (3) By inspiration; (4) By hearing not only the testimony of these angels but the Divine testimony of God Himself!

Surely his faith is now built upon the Rock, and the gates of hell cannot prevail against it!

This is true; and henceforth, we may safely conclude as we follow his career, that not a shadow of doubt of the divinity of Christ's mission ever crosses Peter's mind.

When we think of Peter having been in almost daily contact with the Savior of men, we may conclude that his testimony grew very slowly, but if so, like the oak tree that grows slowly to, it was all the more enduring.

Purity and Sincerity Essentials.

After all, Peter's experience is the experience that will come to nearly all the boys and girls who read these pages. The knowledge of truth, and the testimony of the Gospel may come gradually to most of them. The one great lesson for them to learn even in youth is, that *purity of thought*, and a *sincere heart seeking* the Savior's *guidance daily* will lead to a testimony of the truth of Christ's Gospel as sure and permanent as that which Peter possessed as he descended Mt. Hermon after seeing the transfiguration of Christ, and hearing the voice of God testify to His divinity.

But *knowing* that Jesus is the Savior of mankind, did not give Peter a comprehension of the Gospel plan. In this regard, he had yet much to learn. And, it may be, that his strength of character, or shall we say, his judgment, was not yet so sound as it should have been in a man whose whole life should be as firm as a rock.

In the strength of his testimony, and in a somewhat resigned attitude to the fate that sooner or later was to befall his Master, Peter continued to ask many questions, pertaining to the vital aspects of Christ's mission. One of these which the apostles asked themselves as they came down towards the crowd at the foot of the hill, was, What did the Master mean when He said the Son of Man would rise from the dead?

While the Savior was answering this question, and explaining prophecies relating to it, they came to the place where, the evening before, they had left the other disciples. A great multitude had gathered about them, and the scribes were questioning them.

The Afflicted Boy.

---

[26] Peter 1:7

In the midst of this crowd was a little boy sorely afflicted by an evil spirit. When he was "possessed," he fell to the ground, foamed at the mouth, gnashed his teeth, and pined away. The father met Jesus, and begged Him to relieve his poor boy, and added that the disciples had tried but could not.

"How long a time is it," asked Jesus, "since this came unto him?" "When a child," the father said; "and ofttimes it hath cast him into fire and into the waters, to destroy him, but if thou canst, I ask thee to have compassion on us, and help us."

Jesus rebuked the foul spirit, and the little boy was healed.

A Contrast.

To Peter, James, and John what a contrast was this scene to the one they beheld the night before on the Mount! Here was manifest the power of the evil one, causing suspicions, pain, agony, death; *there* was manifest the power of the Holy One, proclaiming happiness, peace, glory, and immortality! Such have been the results of these two powers as they have influenced the lives of men in all ages. Such is the result today. A vital question for us is, Shall we hover around the foothills of sin where the evil one is triumphant, or shall we at least show a willingness to climb the mount of Holiness and let God transform our lives?

"'Tis not for man to trifle; life is brief,
And sin is here.
Our age is but the falling leaf,
A dropping tear.
We have no time to sport away the hours,
All must be earnest in a world like ours."

LESSON 8 Lessons in True Leadership.

"Character is built out of circumstances. From exactly the same materials one man builds palaces, while another builds hovels."

Between the Transfiguration and the last eventful week of the Savior's life on earth, there are only a few recorded instances in scripture with which Peter is personally mentioned. It is significant, however, that nearly everyone of these, bears either directly or indirectly upon the moulding of Peter's character as an Apostolic leader. Peter knows that Jesus is the Christ that should come, but has he strength to defend Him in word and deed? Does he comprehend the divine principles of the Gospel sufficiently to manifest them in his daily life and conversation and in all his associations with his fellowmen? With the probable exception of the tribute money incident, which emphasized for Peter the divine Sonship of his Master, all the lessons following bear directly upon strength of character and principles of conduct.

TRIBUTE

An Ancient Law.

In those days, there was a tax levied upon every male Jew of twenty years old and upwards for the maintenance of the Temple and its services. This law had been in force ever since the days of the children of Israel when the great lawgiver, Moses, said a "half shekel shall be the offering of the Lord."[27]

Matthew tells us that "When they were come to Capernaum, they that received tribute money, came to Peter and said, "Doth not your Master pay tribute?"[28] "Yes," promptly answered Peter.

If he knew when he was talking to the tax-gatherers, that "there was no money in the bag," he must have wondered how the half-shekel due as tribute could have been paid that day.

Children of the Kingdom Free.

When Peter went back into the house, Jesus anticipated what he was going to say, and asked Him, "Of whom do the kings of the earth take custom or tribute? of their own children, or of strangers?

"Of strangers," answered Peter.

---

[27] Ex. 30:13

[28] Matt. 17:24-27

"Then are the children free," said Jesus, meaning that since this tribute money was for the maintenance of His Father's house, He, the Son, would not have to pay it; but he added:

"Lest we should offend them, go thou to the sea, and cast an hook and take up the fish that first cometh up; and when thou hast opened his mouth, thou shalt find a piece of money: that take and give unto them for me and thee."

This experience must have impressed Peter with the fact that it is better to suffer offense than to give offense.

A LESSON IN FORGIVENESS

About this same time, Peter asked the question:

"Lord, how oft shall my brother sin against me, and I forgive him? Till seven times?"[29]

Perhaps Peter had already been required to settle some difficulty between angry men, or it may be that he had been provoked during a dispute that arose among the disciples as to who was the greatest among them. If some one had taunted him several times about his being the greatest, it is quite probable that his patience was exhausted. At any rate, he wanted to know if there is a limit to the number of times a man should forgive his brother. What a lesson Jesus taught this impetuous apostle when he answered,

"I say not unto thee, until seven times; but until seventy times seven."[30]

Then, to make the teaching more impressive, the Lord told them the parable of the unmerciful debtor.

A certain king took account of his servants for those who had collected his revenue, and found that one owed him ten thousand talents or about fifteen million dollars. This debt the servant could not pay, so the king commanded him to be sold, and his wife and children, and all that he had.[31]

The servant begged for mercy saying, "Lord, have patience with me, and I will pay thee all."

"Then the Lord of that servant was moved with compassion, and loosed him, and forgave him the debt." The master not only had pity for the unfortunate debtor, but freed him from prison, let him keep his wife and children, and cancelled the debt.

The Ungrateful Servant.

---

[29] Matt. 18:21

[30] Matt. 18:22

[31] See II Kings 4:1; Lev. 25:39.

But that same servant went out and found one of his fellow-servants who owed him a hundred pence, more than ten hundred thousand times less than the first servant had owed his master.

Seizing the fellow-servant by the throat and choking him, he demanded, "Pay me that thou owest."

The fellow-servant fell down at his feet and begged for mercy, "Have patience with me and I will pay thee all."

But the unforgiving, merciless servant refusing to give pity, "went and cast him into prison, till he should pay the debt."

So when the Lord heard how the servant whom he had forgiven had treated his fellow-servant, he called that servant back, and said:

"O thou wicked servant! I forgave thee all that debt, because thou desiredst me; should not thou also have had compassion on thy fellow-servant, even as I had pity on thee?"

This unforgiving servant was then told to pay the ten thousand talents, and was delivered over to the "tormentors" until it was all paid.

Then concluded the Savior: "So likewise shall my Heavenly Father do also unto you, if ye from your hearts forgive not every one his brother their trespasses."

Do you think Peter would ever forget that lesson?

THE REWARD OF SACRIFICE

The Rich Young Ruler

One day Peter and others listened to a conversation between their Lord and a rich young ruler. He was a young man, rich, and, as painted by the old masters, very handsome. But with all, he had kept himself morally clean, and desired to get eternal life.[32] But his heart was set upon his riches; so when the Savior said, "Sell all thou hast, and distribute unto the poor, and thou shalt have treasure in heaven, and come, follow me," the young ruler went away very sorrowful.

Then Peter said, "Lo, we have left all and followed thee." As much as to say, Lord we have left everything for Thee, now what shall be our reward? Jesus said:

"There is no man who has left house, or parents, or brethren, or wife, or children, for the kingdom of God's sake, who shall not receive manifold more in this present time; and in the world to come, life everlasting."

"But," He added, "there are many who make themselves first, that shall be last; and the last first."

Humility.

[32] Read Luke 18:18-30.

This last statement must have contained for Peter, the first among the Twelve, an important lesson in Humility.

A LESSON IN FAITH

It was probably on Tuesday of the last week that Jesus spent with His apostles, that Peter called attention to the result of a divine curse.

The Barren Fig Tree.

A day or so before this, Jesus had gone out of His way to get some figs from a tree that stood some distance off. When he found that the tree bore no fruit He said it should never bear fruit again.

On this Tuesday morning as the disciples were passing by, "they saw the fig tree dried up from the roots."

"And Peter calling to remembrance said unto Him, Master, behold the fig tree which Thou cursedst is withered away."

Power of Faith.

Jesus answered: "Have faith in God. For verily I say unto you, that whosoever shall say unto this mountain, Be thou removed, and be thou cast into the sea; and shall not doubt in his heart, but shall believe that those things which he saith shall come to pass; he shall have whatsoever he saith."[33]

On that same day, Peter was undoubtedly with the Twelve on the Mount of Olives when they asked Jesus "privately" about the destruction of the Temple.[34]

Keep Commandments.

To Peter and to all He said: "Watch ye therefore, and pray always, and keep my commandments, that ye may be counted worthy to escape all these things which shall come to pass and to stand before the Son of Man when He shall come clothed in the glory of His Father."

---

[33] Mark 11:22-28

[34] Mark 13; Matt. 24; Luke 21.

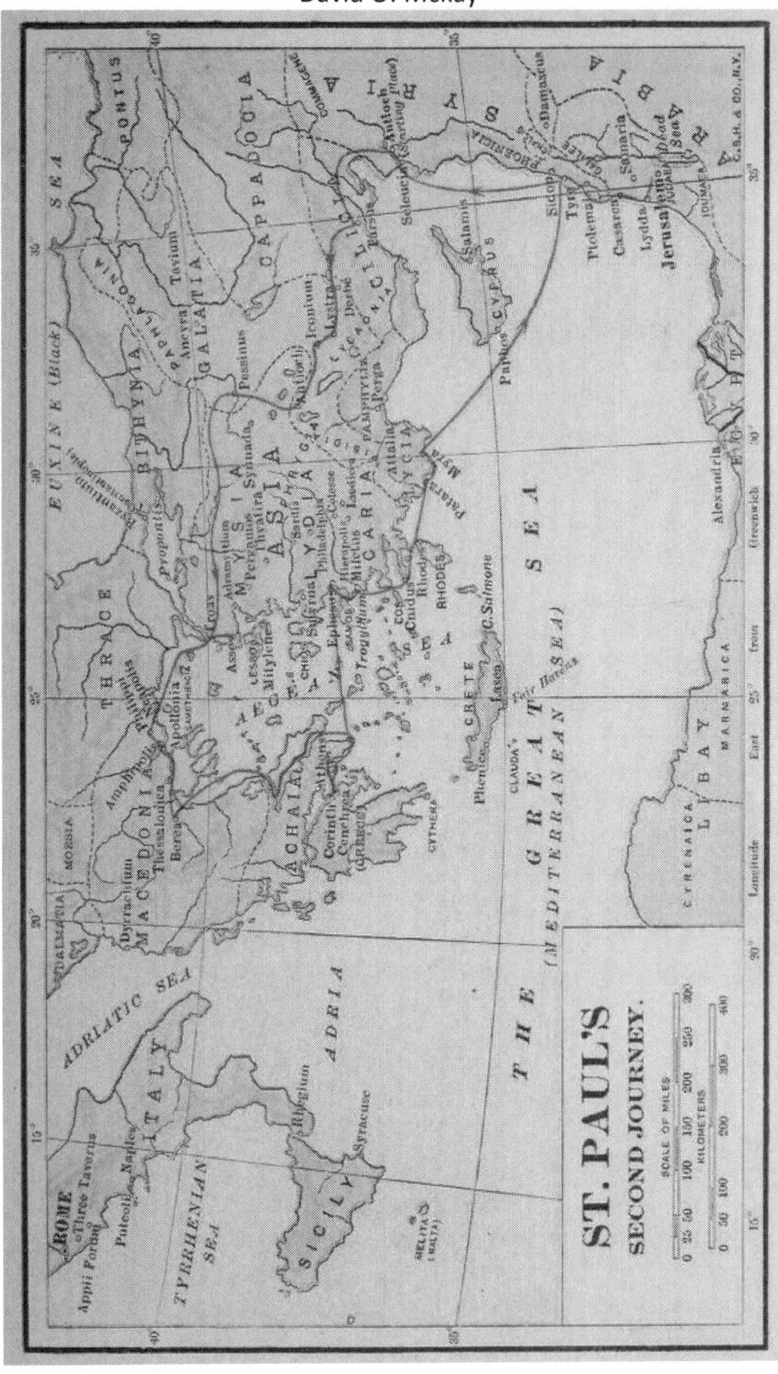
ST. PAUL'S
SECOND JOURNEY.
SCALE OF MILES
KILOMETERS
THE GREAT SEA
(MEDITERRANEAN SEA)
ADRIATIC SEA
ADRIA
TYRRHENIAN SEA
ITALY
SICILY
ROME
Three Taverns
Appii Forum
Puteoli
Naples
Rhegium
Syracuse
MELITA (MALTA)
DALMATIA
MOESIA
MACEDONIA
Dyrrachium
Thessalonica
Berea
Amphipolis
Apollonia
Philippi
THRACE
ACHAIA
Athens
Corinth
Cenchrea
CYTHERA
CRETE
Phenice
Lasea
Fair Havens
C. Salmone
CLAUDA
RHODES
Rhodes
Cnidus
COS
Miletus
Ephesus
Smyrna
Troas
Assos
Mitylene
ASIA
MYSIA
LYDIA
CARIA
LYCIA
Patara
Myra
Attalia
Perga
PAMPHYLIA
Antioch
Iconium
Lystra
Derbe
CILICIA
Tarsus
GALATIA
Ancyra
Tavium
Pessinus
BITHYNIA
PONTUS
CAPPADOCIA
EUXINE (Black) SEA
Byzantium
Propontis
CYPRUS
Salamis
Paphos
SYRIA
Antioch
Seleucia
Damascus
PHOENICIA
Sidon
Tyre
Ptolemais
Caesarea
Samaria
Lydda
Jerusalem
Dead Sea
ARABIA
EGYPT
Alexandria
LIBYA
MARMARICA
CYRENAICA
Longitude East from Greenwich
C.S.H. & CO., N.Y.

LESSON 9 ON THE NIGHT OF THE BETRAYAL

"The weakest spot in every man, is where he thinks himself the wisest."

IN THE UPPER ROOM

On Thursday of the Passion Week, Jesus called Peter and John to Him, and said: "Go, and prepare us the passover, that we may eat."[35]

The Passover.

The Passover, you remember, is the name given to the feast established to commemorate the time when the destroying angel *passed over* the houses of the Hebrews, which had been marked by the blood of the lamb. At this festsival, a lamb was killed, and called the Paschal Lamb. It was on the day that "the passover must be killed" that Peter and John were requested to make preparation.

"Where wilt thou that we prepare?" they asked.

An Upper Room Prepared.

"When ye have entered into the city," replied Jesus, "there shall a man meet you bearing a pitcher of water; follow him into the house where he entereth in. Ask him, Where is the guest chamber, where I shall eat the Passover with my disciples? And he shall show you a large upper room furnished; there make ready."[36]

The two apostles did as they were directed, found everything just as the Lord had stated, and made the necessary preparations.

At the appointed hour Jesus and the Twelve gathered in this upper room. Some think it was in Mark's house, some the house of Joseph of Arimathea, but we do not know, nor does it much matter. We are interested most in what took place there.

A Solemn Meeting.

Jesus sat at the head of the feast. On one side, close enough to recline on His Master's breast sat John, and on the other side sat Peter. It was, perhaps, the most solemn meeting at which the Twelve had ever gathered; for the Savior said at the beginning:

"With desire," that is with longing earnestness, "I have desired to eat this passover with you before I suffer: For I say unto you, I will not any more eat thereof, until it be fulfilled which is written in the prophets concerning me."

---

[35] Luke 22:8

[36] Luke 22:11-12

Meaning that His hour had come when His enemies should take Him and put Him to death.

Near the end of the supper, Jesus rose from where He was reclining, laid aside His outer garments, took a towel and tied it around His waist, thus assuming a servant's dress. He then took a basin of water and proceeded to wash the disciples' feet.

Jesus Washeth Disciples' Feet.

It may be that the Savior had detected in the minds of some the same thought which had caused a dispute among them once before, as to who was the greatest among them. Perhaps this thought arose when they saw Peter and John occupying the places of honor. At any rate, their Lord, the greatest among them, assumed the attitude of servant, the least and humblest of them all.

Peter Objects.

When He came to Peter, the latter said: "Lord, dost *Thou* wash *my* feet?" Peter would serve his Master, but his Master must never serve him!

"What I do thou knowest not now: but thou shalt know hereafter," answered Jesus.

"Thou needst not to wash my feet."

"If I wash thee not," continued Jesus, "thou hast no part with me."

When Peter thought that his refusal to submit to be served by the Lord, was really putting the Savior away from him, he said,

"Lord, not my feet only, but also my hands and my head."

An Example.

"So after He had washed their feet, and had taken his garments, and was set down again. He said unto them: Know ye what I have done to you? Ye call me Master and Lord; and ye say well, for so I am. If I then, your Lord and Master, have washed your feet; ye also ought to wash one another's feet. For I have given you an example, that ye should do as I have done to you."

Thus did these twelve men receive in an impressive and practical manner, the divine lesson of service. Thus did they learn that those who were greatest among them were really the servants of all. Indeed, in the Church of Christ, there are no masters and no servants, but all working for every one and each one for all.

"One of You Shall Betray Me."

Immediately following this impressive and sacred ceremony, the full significance of which very few understand, the Savior said, "One of you shall betray me."

This announcement cast a gloom over all. To make it caused "trouble" to come over Christ's "spirit;" and to hear it, made all "exceeding sorrowful."[37]

They began to inquire among themselves which one of them should be so faithless; and soon each asked the Master, "Lord, is it I?"

Judas, last of all answered and said, "Lord, is it I?"

Jesus' answer, "Thou hast said," must not have been heard by the others, because Peter beckoned to John to ask the Master "who it should be of whom he spoke."

Jesus replied, also in a quiet manner, "He it is, to whom I shall give a sop, when I have dipped it."

Judas Iscariot.

When he had dipped the sop, he handed it to Judas Iscariot. Peter and John, then, knew who the traitor was; but the others probably did not; for they wondered what Jesus meant when He said to Judas: "That thou doest do quickly."

LOYALTY AS PETER FELT IT

After the traitor went out into the night—oh such a night for him! Jesus continued to teach and to comfort the Eleven.

Love One Another.

"A new commandment I give unto you," He said, "That ye love one another; as I have loved you, that ye also love one another."

Among other things, He said, referring to His approaching death, "Whither I go ye cannot come."

This stirred Peter's love and he inquired, "Lord, why cannot I follow Thee now? I will lay down my life for Thy sake."[38]

Peter to Be Tried.

"Simon, Simon, behold Satan hath desired you that he may sift you as wheat. But I have prayed for thee that thy faith fail not; and when thou art converted, [that is, "brought back afresh as a penitent disciple"] strengthen thy brethren."[39]

This grieved Peter very deeply. To think that his Master would even suspect that he, *Peter*, would even weaken in his steadfastness to

---

[37] Matt. 26:22

[38] John 13:34-37

[39] Luke 22:31, 32.

his Lord! (It is significant that the Lord called him by his old name, *Simon*).

Peter protested, saying, "Lord, I am ready to go with thee, both into prison, and to death."[40]

A Prophecy.

"I tell you, Peter," continued the Savior, "that the cock shall not crow this day, before that thou shalt thrice deny that thou knowest me."

But, he spake the more vehemently. "Though I should die with thee, yet will I not deny thee. Likewise so said they all."[41]

Peter meant every word he said, and he felt deeply the truth of what he spake; but his real strength had not come to him yet, and his Master knew it. It would come but it would be "Born in the deep silence of a long-suffering heart."

LOYALTY AS PETER ACTED IT

Gethsemane.

Later in the night, the company left the upper room, crossed the brook Kedron, and went to the Garden of Gethsemane, on the west side of the Mount of Olives.

Bidding eight of the Eleven to remain together. He took the other three, Peter, James, and John, apart. His soul "was exceeding sorrowful even unto death."

He said, "Tarry ye here, and watch with me."

"Not My Will but Thine be Done."

Soon He withdrew a little from them, and prayed. The Apostles could see Him, perhaps could hear Him, as He cried, "Father, if it be possible let this cup pass; nevertheless not my will, but thine be done."

When he returned, and found the three sleeping, He said, "Simon [Simon again] sleepest thou? Couldst not thou watch one hour?"

"Watch ye and pray, lest ye enter into temptation."

"The spirit truly is ready, but the flesh is weak."[42]

Peter and His Brethren Drowsy.

A second time He withdrew; a second time returned; a second time found them sleeping; "for their eyes were heavy; neither knew they what to answer Him."

---

[40] Luke 22:33

[41] Matt. 26:35

[42] Mark 14:38

When He returned the third time, He said kindly, "Sleep on now and take your rest; it is enough, the hour is come; behold the Son of Man is betrayed into the hands of sinners."

After a little longer sleep, the three were awakened by Jesus, only to see approaching "a great multitude, with swords and staves, from the chief priests, and the scribes and the elders." At their head was Judas who approached his Lord, and betrayed Him with a kiss.

Peter Defends His Lord.

As soldiers went to lay hands upon Jesus, Peter, who was now thoroughly aroused, jumped to the rescue of his Master, "drew his sword, and smote a servant of the high priest and cut off his ear."

This servant, whose right ear Peter struck off with one blow, was called Malchus.

A Lesson.

"Put up thy sword into the sheath," commanded the Savior, "the cup which my Father hath given me, shall I not drink it?" What a lesson to Peter! Even though duty led to suffering and death, yet would the Lord not waver in His strength.

Then said Jesus, "Suffer ye thus far, and He touched his ear and healed him."[43]

As the officers led Jesus away, the disciples "all forsook Him, and fled."

Peter Follows Jesus.

Peter's strength and loyalty were wavering; but he could not bring himself to flee with the others. Neither could he conclude that it was best to go with Jesus; so he did neither, but "followed Him afar off, even unto the palace of the high priest."

At first, he remained on the outside, but later ventured in where the servants were sitting.

WEAKNESS BRINGS MISERY

While Peter was standing by the stove warming himself, a girl came in, and recognizing him as one who had been with Jesus, said, "Thou, also wast with Jesus of Galilee."

In a Moment of Weakness.

"I know not what thou sayest," said Peter before them all.

He then stepped out on the porch, perhaps to cool his burning conscience or to try to collect himself to know what best to do.

---

[43] Luke 22:51

A man seeing him there cried out, "This man was also with Jesus of Nazareth."

"I do not know the man," said Simon; and this time he took an oath.

One of the servants of the high priest, who was related to Malchus approached Peter a little later, and said, "Did I not see thee in the Garden with Him?"[44]

Then began he to curse and to swear, saying, "Man, I know not what thou sayest." At that moment, Peter heard the cock crow.

Sorrow.

Almost immediately, too, the Savior passing near him, "turned and looked upon Peter." Then recalling the words of his Lord, "Before the cock crow twice, thou shalt deny me thrice."[45] Peter went out and wept bitterly.

---

[44] John 18:26

[45] Luke 22:61

LESSON 10 OUT OF GLOOM, INTO LIGHT

"Strength is born in the deep silence of long-suffering hearts, not amidst joy."

Out of Weakness, Strength.

It is said when Peter "went out speechless from the face of all, * * * and filled the silence, weeping bitterly," that his grief was so heavy that he remained alone all day during Friday and Saturday following the Savior's crucifixion. If so, his sorrow for what he had done was made all the more acute as he recalled the many kind words the Savior had spoken to him, and the many, many happy moments he had spent in the Lord's company. Every word and act and look associated with his Master would flash upon his mind with a new meaning. Perhaps for the first time in his life, he now fully realized why the Lord had desired his nature and faith to be as "The Rock." Through the mist of his bitter tears, he saw all the true attributes of manhood as they were personified in Jesus—Reverence, Brotherliness, Patience, Sincerity, Courage. These and many other noble traits made Jesus appear to him now more holy than ever. But the more clearly Peter saw Christ's strength and holiness, the more clearly he realized his own littleness and misery. This last manifestation of his weakness, which led him to deny his Lord, made him see himself in a new light, and it had a decisive effect upon him. Out of the "deep silence" of his suffering, those two days, there was born that strength which Christ had urged upon him ever since He called him "Peter."

A Sad Meeting.

It must have been a sad meeting when John and Peter first came together after the Crucifixion. When it was or where, we are not told; but we are sure that John must have recognized a great change in his fellow-apostle. Out of the haggard look and the deep lines of grief there must have shone a humility which John had never before seen in Peter's face. We can only imagine what Peter's feelings were as he listened to John tell of all that had happened before Herod and Pilate, and at the Cross. Mingling with Peter's grief was the keen disappointment that their Messiah, their King, was not to free the Jews and rule over them as he had hoped. In doubt as to what to do, they probably decided to visit the place where their Master had been laid, and then return to their former vocation as fishermen.

At the Sepulchre.

But there was one whose love and devotion took her to the tomb even before the Apostles. Mary Magdalene, "while it was yet dark" approached the place where she thought Jesus slept in death. But instead of seeing her Lord's body in the cold, dark sepulchre, around which there was nothing but gloom and sorrow, she found an empty tomb. In alarm, she ran to Peter and John, and breathlessly cried, "They have taken away the Lord out of the sepulchre." "Peter therefore went forth, and that other disciple, and came to the sepulchre." At first, they ran together, but Peter already weary with suffering, was soon out-distanced by the younger Apostle John, who reached the place first.

"And stooping down, and looking in, he saw the linen clothes lying; yet went he not in."

Just to look in, however, did not satisfy Peter; for as soon as he came, he "went into the sepulchre." John followed him. They noticed the napkin that had been on Jesus' head wrapped and placed by itself; the linen clothes, too, were folded neatly and placed aside with care. They concluded that thieves would not have done this, and so dispelled Mary's theory that the Lord's body had been stolen. But "as yet they knew not the scripture that He must rise again from the dead."

Mary Beholds Risen Redeemer.

Filled with wonder and perplexity, the two disciples "went away again to their own home," but Mary lingered near the tomb, and as a reward for her faithfulness and devotion, became the first person in the world to behold the risen Redeemer.

Peter Sees His Lord.

Other women who came to the tomb that morning to render, as they thought, the last slight service to their Lord, were permitted also to see Him. Later on that same day, it seems that He appeared to Peter; but where, or under what circumstances, or what was said, we do not know. We may rest assured, however, that Peter's repentant soul was filled with joy eternal as he received the divine forgiveness of His Lord.

Disciples From Emmans.

That evening as the Eleven were assembled in a room talking over the events of the day, and particularly the Lord's appearance to Peter, there entered two disciples from Emmaus. They were no sooner in the presence of the Eleven, than they heard the joyous message, "The Lord is risen indeed and hath appeared unto Simon." They could readily believe this, for they said, "When we were returning from Jerusalem, today, after having heard of the angels and the empty tomb, Jesus Himself drew near and went with us."

Jesus Appears to Eleven.

While they were thus assembled, Jesus appeared to them again, "and saith unto them. Peace be unto you." Such scenes as that cannot be described, and the evangelists who tell us about it simply state the fact and leave us to imagine what their thoughts and feelings were on that glorious occasion. We are sure, though, that we can say of Peter as has been written of the Prophet Joseph when he, too, saw the Savior,

"O what rapture filled his bosom,
For he saw the living God."

THE FISHERMAN BECOMES THE SHEPHERD

On Sea of Tiberias.

Several days after this, Peter and six other disciples were back on the sea of Tiberias, fishing. They were in Galilee, evidently waiting to meet the Lord there as He had promised. One evening, as if Peter had almost despaired of waiting, he said to the others,

"I'm going a fishing."

"We also go with thee," said they.

They entered into a boat immediately, and let down their nets. They toiled all night, and caught nothing, just as some of them had done on a memorable occasion several months before.

As morning dawned, they saw a man standing on the shore, but in the distance, they could not tell who he was. Suddenly the man cried,

"Sirs, have ye any meat?"

"No," was their reply.

Many Fish Caught.

"Cast the net on the right side of the ship and ye shall find," said the man.

They did so, and caught so many fish that they could scarcely draw in the net.

John, whose loving eyes were made more keen by a loving heart, rushed to Peter's side and whispered, "It is the Lord."

Instantly, Peter knew John spoke the truth, and man of action that he was, he put on his fisherman's coat, plunged into the sea, and hastened to the feet of his Master. The others came in the little ship, dragging the net of fishes.

Jesus had already started a fire, and' was cooking them something to eat. After the greetings, He said, "Bring of the fish which ye have now caught."

Peter was the leader in going to the net and in drawing it to the land. While the fish were cooking, the disciples counted the number caught, and found that in that one draught there were one hundred and fifty-three: "and for all there were so many, yet was the net not broken."

Peter a Shepherd of Christ's Fold.

Jesus had shown them where to catch the fish, He had started the fire on which to cook them, and now "He taketh the bread and giveth them and the fish likewise." Surely these little incidents would tend to impress them with the truth that if they "would seek first the Kingdom of God and His righteousness all else will be added." At any rate, this is the lesson taught on that great occasion: The apostles were not now to spend their lives seeking the things which perish, but in searching for souls that will endure throughout all eternity. Many are now together in the fold of Christ, and the shepherd is called away. Henceforward Peter and his associates must be the keepers of this flock.

When they had broken their fast, Jesus said to Simon Peter, "Simon, son of Jonas, lovest thou me more than these?"

"Yea, Lord," answered Peter, "Thou knowest that I love Thee."

"Feed my lambs." That is, Take care of the little ones in my Church. Do not let them go astray in paths that will lead them to sin and misery.

He saith unto him again the second time,

"Simon, son of Jonas lovest thou me?"

"Yea, Lord, Thou knowest that I love Thee."

"Feed my sheep." Keep the older ones together and give them the words of life as thou hast received them from me.

A third time Jesus said,

"Simon, son of Jonas, lovest thou me?"

And Peter, somewhat grieved, answered, "Lord, thou knowest all things; Thou knowest that I love Thee."

"Feed my sheep."

Duty First.

And then the Savior admonished Peter not always to follow his own inclinations, and impulsive nature; but ever to do his duty as the Shepherd of the Fold. When Peter was young, and did not have the knowledge and responsibility he now possessed, he could go fishing, and make money, or study, or do whatever he wished, but now he must attend to his duties in the Kingdom of God no matter what might come to him personally in doing so. Even though Peter's duty led to the cross, the Savior said, "Follow me."

While this conversation was going on, Jesus and Peter were walking alone a little ahead of the others. Peter turned, and saw John following close to them.

"Lord," said Peter, "what is John to do?"

"If I will that he tarry till I come, what is that to thee, follow thou me." As much as to say, Just attend faithfully to your duty, Peter, teach others to do the same, and all will be well.

This is the last recorded word of Christ to Peter; but he was present of course when the Savior gave His final charge to the Twelve.[46]

From this time Peter's zeal in the Work of the Ministry was constant, and his boldness unsubdued.

---

[46] Mark 16:16

LESSON 11 A TRUE LEADER AND VALIANT DEFENDER

"The reward of one's duty done is the power to do another."

With a knowledge that Jesus Christ was his Savior, that he was happiest when he did what his Lord wanted him to do, and that when he did wrong or yielded to the influence of evil men, he was miserable, Peter, began his great mission as chief apostle and president of the Twelve.

In Jerusalem.

In accordance with the Savior's command "that they should not depart from Jerusalem" until they received the Holy Ghost, for some time after the Lord's ascension, made his home in the Holy City. Here he and James and John, and others of the Eleven, frequently met in an upper room, perhaps the same room in which Jesus had eaten the Passover with His disciples. With them were Mary, the Mother of Jesus, and some other women.

AN APOSTLE CHOSEN

A New Apostle Chosen.

On one of these occasions, there were present one hundred and twenty people, "all engaged in prayer and supplication." Peter arose in their midst and said it was necessary to choose a man who had been faithful in following the Savior to take the place of the traitor, Judas, in the Quorum of Twelve Apostles. There were two names suggested, Joseph called Barsabas, and Matthias. Knowing that the Lord should choose the men who were to be His special witnesses, they prayed, saying, "Thou, Lord, who knowest the hearts of all men, show whither of these two Thou hast chosen." Then they "gave forth their lots; and the lot fell upon Matthias; and he was numbered with the eleven apostles."

THE DAY OF PENTECOST

The Holy Ghost.

Before nine o'clock in the morning, ten days after the Saviors' ascension, and fifty days after the Passover associated with the crucifixion, the apostles held a memorable meeting. As they sat "with one acord in one place" "suddenly there came a sound from heaven as of a rushing mighty wind, and it filled all the house where they were sitting." Thus came the baptism by fire and the Holy Ghost as Christ had promised. The Comforter about which their Master had so often spoken had at length come to them, to guide and to inspire them as Jesus had done in person.

The Gift of Tongues.

Immediately a wonderful manifestation took place. Though nearly all the apostles were Galileans and spoke the same language, yet when they began to bear testimony of Christ and His Gospel, they "began to speak with other tongues as the spirit gave them utterance."

That a remarkable thing had occurred was soon noised about the city, and people in great numbers gathered around the apostles. In the crowd were Jews from many nations who had come to Jerusalem to celebrate Pentecost. These spoke the language of the country from which they came. Imagine their amazement when every one heard the Gospel preached in his own tongue!

"Are not theses men who speak Galileans?" they asked. "Yes," was the answer.

"Then how hear we every man in his own tongue, wherein we were born?"

As the apostles, one after another, told of the salvation of man through the Gospel of Jesus Christ, some of the people were amazed, and some amused, but all were perplexed.

"What does this mean?" asked some.

"They act as though they are drunken," said others.

Then Peter arose, and, in mighty power, addressed the multitude. "Ye men of Judea," he began, "and all ye that dwell at Jerusalem; be this known unto you, and hearken to my words:

Peter's Address.

"For these are not drunken as ye suppose, seeing it is but the third hour of the day.

"But this is what was spoken by the Prophet Joel."[47]

Undoubtedly only a small part of Peter's address is given to us; but as we read his inspired words, and partake of the fearlessness with which he told the Jews that they had crucified the Christ, we readily become convinced that the weakness he manifested about a month and a half before, has been replaced by the strength of the man of God. Then he stammered and swore, "I know not the man;" *now*, he declared, "This Jesus hath God raised up, whereof, we are all witnesses."

His Fearlessness.

---

[47] Read the entire address as recorded in Acts 2:14-37

With all the courage of his convictions, and with the power of the Holy Ghost, he added: "Therefore, let all the house of Israel know assuredly, God hath made that same Jesus, whom ye have crucified, both Lord and Christ."

As they heard of the wickedness in crucifying the Christ and of many other sins, they desired to get forgiveness for what they had done, and cried out to Peter—and the other apostles,

"Men and brethren, what shall we do?"

"What Shall We Do?"

In Peter's answer, we see the open door through which all must pass who desire to be saved in the Kingdom of God:

"Repent and be baptized, everyone of you, in the name of Jesus Christ, for the remission of your sins, and ye shall receive the gift of the Holy Ghost."

Then those who believed what Peter had said, were baptized; and the little band of one hundred and twenty grew that day to three thousand one hundred and twenty. And every day thereafter, many others became converted, and joined the Church.

THE MAN WHO HAD NEVER WALKED.

The General Meeting Place.

About three o'clock one afternoon Peter and John were going up to the Temple to pray. Here they came every day to meet in one accord with the saints, and then visit "from house to house; breaking bread." Thus the Temple seems to have been the general meeting place for the first followers of the Redeemer. It was His house, and there they liked to gather to worship. The main entrance to the Temple was by way of "Solomon's Porch" through a gate that was called "The beautiful Gate." Here gathered all the poor people—the blind, the lame, the weak, and those who were diseased—who lived by asking alms from those who came to the Temple.

An Appeal.

On this particular afternoon, one of these made his piteous appeal to Peter and John. He was a man forty years old, but he had never taken a step in his life. Friends would carry him there in the morning, and then carry him home at night. In answer to his request for money, Peter said, "Look on us."

The Answer.

While the man was wondering how much money the apostles would give him, Peter added, "Silver and gold have I none: but such as I have, give I thee: in the name of Jesus Christ of Nazareth, rise up and walk."

Taking him by the right hand, Peter lifted him up, and immediately his feet and ankle bones received strength.

The man was so happy that he went into the Temple leaping and praising God for the great miracle that had come into his life.

Again the people were "filled with wonder and amazement," and gathered in great numbers in "Solomon's Porch" staring at Peter and John, wondering what kind of men they were.

Another Powerful Address.

Here Peter gave another great address in which he said that this man was healed through faith in the name of Jesus Christ "whom God hath glorified, whom ye delivered up and denied Him in the presence of Pilate, when he was determined to let Him go.

"But ye denied the Holy One and the Just, and desired a murderer to be granted unto you; and killed the Prince of Life, whom God hath raised from the dead; whereof we are witnesses."[48]

[48] Read Acts 3:2-26

LESSON 12 PETER AND JOHN ARRESTED

"As no good is done, or spoken, or thought by any man without the assistance of God, * * * so there is no evil done, or spoken, or thought without the assistance of the devil."

Peter Interrupted.

While Peter was still preaching to the thousands assembled in "Solomon's Porch," he saw approaching from the castle near the Temple, the captain of the guard and his band.

The Jewish priests had become jealous, and suspicious of the apostles, and looked with alarm at the thousands of people joining the Church. So they decided to call out the soldiers, disperse the multitude, and arrest Peter and John as the men responsible for all the excitement. However, about five thousand of the people were converted that afternoon.

Imprisoned.

So the soldiers "laid hands on them," and put them in jail, "For it was now eventide," and, therefore, too late to take them to trial. Though they were shut up in close cells, yet their spirits were free and their consciences clear. They could sleep more peacefully than the priest who had caused their arrest.

Before the Sanhedrin.

In the morning, the prisoners were taken to the Sanhedrin where sat Annas, the high priest and Caiaphas, and John and Alexander, and relatives of the high priest. These men had condemned Jesus, perhaps in this very room, and they were determined that the preaching in the name of Jesus of Nazareth must cease.

Others were present that morning, and among them true friends to the apostles. One of these was the lame man, who had been healed.

Curiosity and Amazement.

As he was the innocent cause of the multitude's gathering the previous evening, everybody seemed to be even more interested in him than in the prisoners. He was carried, they knew, only twenty-four hours ago, to the temple gate, and now they see him walking firmly through the crowd to get near the apostles.

"By what power, or by what name, have ye done this?" demanded one of the judges.

"Then Peter, filled with the Holy Ghost, said unto them. Ye rulers of the people, and elders of Israel,

"If we this day be examined of the good deed done to the impotent man, by what means he is made whole;

Peter Testifies of Christ.

"Be it known unto you all, and unto all the people of Israel, that by the name of Jesus of Nazareth whom ye crucified, whom God raised from the dead, even by Him doth this man stand here before you whole."

How those sinful men must have quailed as they beheld Peter's dignity, felt his sincerity, and listened to the flashing words that pierced their guilty souls!

He told them further that they could get no salvation unless they, too, took upon themselves the name of Christ: "for there is none other name under heaven given among men, whereby we must be saved."

What could the priests say? What could they do?

Nothing.

Enemies Confounded.

There stood the man sound and whole, who had been helpless for forty years!

There stood Peter boldly proclaiming that the miracle was wrought in the name of Jesus of Nazareth whom they had condemned to death.

They considered Peter unlearned, but he had confounded them all.

Counsel.

After ordering the prisoners to be taken into another room, they said among themselves:

"What shall we do to these men? for that indeed a notable miracle hath been done by them is manifest to all them that dwell in Jerusalem and we cannot deny it."

So, in order that the doctrine the apostles were preaching would spread no further, they concluded to threaten Peter and John, and command them not to speak to any man in "this name."

So they called the prisoners back and said in effect; "You must never more speak at all, nor teach in the name of Jesus."

Better to Obey God Than Man.

Said the apostles, "Whether it be right in the sight of God, to hearken unto you more than unto God, judge ye.

"For we cannot but speak the things which we have seen and heard."

No doubt these priests would have punished the apostles then, if they had not been afraid of the people, all of whom "Glorified God for that which was done."

When they were let go, Peter and John went "to their own company," and told their friends all that had happened. When they heard it, the saints united in a prayer of thanksgiving to God for all His blessings unto them.[49]

At this meeting there was another mighty manifestation of the Holy Ghost, "and they spake the word of God with boldness."

DANGERS WITHIN THE FOLD

Unconverted.

But these leaders had to contend not only with enemies outside the Church but with the scheming, dishonest people who stole their way into the fold. There were men and women who had not repented of their sins before they were baptized; so they did not receive the Holy Ghost.

Two of these were Ananias and his wife Sapphira.

Everybody who joined the Church had everything in common. Those who had land and other property sold it and brought the money to the apostles. There were no rich and no poor—all had everything that anybody else had, and everyone possessed what belonged to all.

Two Deceivers.

Ananias and Sapphira sold a possession; but they brought only part of the money, and said it was all. Thus they told a falsehood, and showed themselves to be among the worst people in the world; for,

The Lie Detected.

"Who dares think one thing,
And another tell,
My soul detests him,
As the gates of hell."

Through the inspiration of the Holy Spirit, Peter detected the lie, and said to Ananias,

"Why hath Satan filled thine heart to lie to the Holy Ghost, and to keep back part of the price of the land?"

"Why hast thou conceived this thing in thine heart?

---

[49] See Acts 4:23-31

A Severe Punishment.

"Thou hast not lied unto me, but unto God."

"And Ananias hearing these words fell down and gave up the ghost."

About three hours later, his wife came in, and told the same story as her husband. She, too, received a divine rebuke, and paid the penalty of her sin by giving up her life.

After that, no one dare try to deceive the apostles in giving gifts to the Church.

This is a good lesson for all to keep in mind today especially when paying tithing to the Lord.

PETER.
"They brought forth the sick into the streets, and laid them on beds and couches, that at least the shadow of Peter passing by might overshadow some of them."

LESSON 13 PERSECUTED BUT UNDISMAYED

"Dinna curse him, sir; I have heard it said that a curse was a stone flung up to the heavens, and most likely to return on the head of him that sent it."

The earnestness with which Peter and the other Apostles preached the Gospel of Jesus Christ had a wonderful effect upon the multitudes who heard them. At Solomon's Porch, day after day, men and women heard the Twelve testify that the Redeemer of the world had indeed come.

Sick Healed.

These testimonies were corroborated, too, by wonderful manifestations; for "by the hands of the Apostles were many signs and wonders wrought among the people." So great was the faith in the power of God that "they brought forth the sick into the streets, and laid them on beds and couches, that at the least the shadow of Peter passing by might overshadow some of them."

Nor were the sick in Jerusalem the only persons blessed; but people from the villages near Jerusalem who were sick and afflicted with evil spirits appealed to the Apostles, and by the power of God, were healed.

Rejoicing and Unity.

It must have given Peter and his fellow Apostles much cause for rejoicing to see the interest and the faith of so many thousands in the message of Christ. What rejoicing, too, in the hearts of all those invalids, who, made well, leaped from their couches and joined in the praises of the Redeemer!

How the Twelve must have loved each other and their hearts beat as one as, day after day, they bore witness to the death and the resurrection of their Lord, and received divine assurances that He was still manifesting Himself to them through the Holy Ghost! As this Spirit permeated those who joined the Church, no wonder that "the multitude of them that believed were of one heart and of one soul."

Hatred.

But there were some men in Jerusalem who were made very jealous of the Apostles, and whose hearts were filled, not with rejoicing but envy. These were the men who had been the leaders in crucifying Jesus. It is said that "No sooner is a temple built to God, but the devil builds a chapel hard by;" thus while the Lord was pouring out the Spirit of love upon those who joined the Church, the devil was pouring hate into the hearts of those who were wicked and would not repent.

Peter Imprisoned.

So, "the high priest rose up, and all they that were with him, and, being filled with envy, laid their hands on the Apostles, and put them in the common prison." These prejudiced and ignorant rulers were determined to make the Twelve stop preaching Christ; because if what the Twelve said was true, these rulers would be blamed for having put to death the King of the Jews. But poor, puny man cannot hinder the work of the Lord.

A Miraculous Deliverance.

Some time during the night while the prisoners were together in the prison room—perhaps singing hymns and praying—an angel of the Lord appeared to them. He opened the prison doors, brought them out, and said:

"Go, stand and speak in the temple to the people all the words of this life."

About this command George L. Weed writes:

"'Go'—the very word they had heard from the Lord before His ascension to Heaven, whence He had sent His angel to repeat it in prison. 'Go'—in spite of threats and commands, of bolts and bars and prison guards. In the name of Him who commanded you, 'Go, preach my Gospel,' do ye 'Stand and speak in the Temple'—the very place whence ye have been driven, Speak to the people, all who will listen, for your Master and mine is the Savior of them all. Speak all the words of this life—the promised future life of which the resurrection of Jesus is the first fulfilment."

Obedient to the angel's command, the Twelve entered into the temple early in the morning, and taught. How their message must have thrilled the eager listeners who had assembled that early to hear the word of God!

The Jews Perplexed.

Just as early that same morning another group of men assembled. The high priest called his council together, "and all the senate of the children of Israel." When this council was in readiness, the high priest sent to the prison for Peter and his brethren. Soon the officers returned and said:

"The prison truly found we shut with all safety, and the keepers standing without before the doors: but when we had opened, we found no man within."

Perplexed by this unexpected anouncement, the high priest and council seemed to be unable to decide just what to do. While they were still seeking for a satisfactory explanation or for the next definite step to take, some one entered, saying:

"Behold, the men whom ye put in prison are standing in the temple, and teaching the people."

Hearing this, the captain of the temple with his officers fetched the Apostles before the council. But the officers took them "without violence;" that is, without doing them any injury or without using them roughly; "for they feared the people, lest they should have been stoned."

As soon as the Twelve appeared, the high priest demanded:

Before the Council.

"Did not we straitly command you that ye should not teach in this name? and behold, ye have filled Jerusalem with your doctrine, and intend to bring this man's blood upon us."

His prejudiced heart prompts him to speak of Jesus without mentioning His name. But even in his bitterness, he bears a noted testimony of the success of the Apostles' preaching. "Ye have filled Jerusalem with your doctrine," said he, "and now intend to bring this man's blood upon us." Did the high priest remember, just then, that the Jews cried at the trial of Jesus, "His blood be upon us, and upon our children?" If so, he must have felt fearful that the imprecation might be realized.

Then said Peter and the other Apostles:

"We ought to obey God rather than men." Manifesting as much eagerness as the high priest had shown reluctance to name Jesus, Peter added:

A Bold Speech.

"The God of our fathers raised up Jesus, whom ye slew and hanged on a tree.

"Him hath God exalted with his right hand to be a Prince and a Savior, for to give repentance to Israel, and forgiveness of sins. We testify to these things and the Holy Ghost also says they are true."

This bold speech cut the wicked judges to the heart. It made them so angry that they talked of slaying the Twelve, just as they had killed the Savior.

Gamaliel's Defense.

But there was one able lawyer among them who had justice in his heart. His name was Gamaliel. He stood up among them and said:

"Put these men out of the hall for a little space."

When this was done, he continued, in effect:

"Ye men of Israel, be careful what you do to these men. If what they are preaching is of man it will soon pass away, just as Theudas and about four hundred who joined him were scattered and brought to naught; and just as Judas of Galilee and those who believed in him were dispersed.

"But if it be of God, ye cannot overthrow it; lest haply ye be found even to fight against God."[50]

Beaten and Released.

Gamaliel's influence prevailed; and the Apostles' lives were spared; but they were not released until they had been beaten and commanded not to speak in the name of Jesus. If the beating they received was a scourging, each man was stripped to the waist, his arms tied to a low pillar, that he might lean forward, so the whipping could more easily strike him, and he was given thirty-nine lashes.

As the Twelve, bleeding from the wounds of the lash, left the council chamber, their hearts were filled, not with sorrow and regret, but with rejoicing "that they were counted worthy to suffer shame for His name."

[50] Read the text: Acts 5:33-39

LESSON 14 A SPECIAL VISIT TO SAMARIA

Deacons.

As the membership of the Church increased, men were called and ordained to various offices in the work of the ministry. Besides the Apostles, there were Evangelists, Pastors, Teachers, Deacons, etc. Among the first to be chosen and ordained to a particular office of service in the Church were "seven men of honest report, full of the Holy Ghost and wisdom." Their names were, Stephen, Philip, Prochorus, Nicanor, Timon, Parmenas, and Nicolas. They are called Deacons and one of their chief duties was to oversee the distribution of food among the poor.

Stephen Martyred.

Shortly after their appointment, a bitter and cruel persecution arose against the Church at Jerusalem during which the Saints were scattered abroad throughout the regions of Judea, and Samaria. Stephen, "a man full of faith and of the Holy Ghost," was stoned to death. Philip went down to the city of Samaria, and there continued to preach Christ unto the Samaritans.

Philip.

It seems that great power accompanied Philip's ministry, for "unclean spirits, crying with loud voice, came out of many that were possessed; and many taken with palsies, and that were lame, were healed. And there was great joy in that city." The people, "with one accord," heeded Philip's message and were baptized into the Church.

Authority Limited.

But baptism by water is not sufficient. It must be followed by the baptism of the Holy Ghost. It seems, however, that Philip, though he had authority to baptize, did not have the right to confer the Holy Ghost. He, therefore, probably held the office of Priest.

Holy Ghost Given.

When the news that Samaria had received the Gospel reached Jerusalem, "Peter and John were sent unto them. Who, when they were come down, prayed for them that they might receive the Holy Ghost." On the heads of these baptized believers, Peter and John then laid their hands and conferred upon them the Holy Ghost.

Pretenders.

The Lord does not accept everyone who is baptized into the Church. Only those who sincerely believe in Jesus Christ as the Redeemer of the World and who repent of their sins receive the Holy Ghost. Those who are baptized without faith and repentance are mere pretenders.

One such joined the Church in England a few years ago. One day a member seeing that the young man had no faith, asked him why he had joined the Church.

"Oh, just to get out to America," he replied.

A little later in the conversation, he confessed to having joined the Catholic Church, at one time, to get a string of beads! and afterward joined the Latter-day Saints to come to Utah. Of course, it was not long before he was excommunicated, and soon after fell into the depths of sin and misery.

Simon the Sorcerer.

At the time Philip went to Samaria, there was a man named Simon in the city, who was a great pretender. He claimed to be a sorcerer, and made a great deal of money by bewitching people with his sorceries. However, when the people heard the true Gospel, and saw miracles wrought by the power of God, they lost interest in Simon's sorceries, and were baptized by Philip.

ST. PETER AND ST. JOHN IN SAMARIA.
"On the heads of these baptized believers, Peter and John then laid their hands, and conferred upon them the Holy Ghost."

"Then Simon himself believed also; and when he was baptized, he continued with Philip, and wondered, beholding the signs and great miracles which were done." But he was not converted. His only purpose of joining the Church was to find out how these miracles were performed, thinking he might use them for gain.

His Greed.

When Simon saw that through the laying on of the Apostles' hands the Holy Ghost was given, he offered them money, saying, "Give me also this power, that on whomsoever I lay hands, he may receive the Holy Ghost." Poor, greedy man! His lust for gold led him to sacrifice even his honor!

"And hence one master passion in the breast,
Like Aaron's serpent, swallows up the rest."

Simon Rebuked.

If he thought Peter's heart was as avaricious as his own, he soon learned better, for the indignant Apostle, looking straight into the sordid soul of this mercenary hypocrite, answered:

"Thy money perish with thee, because thou hast thought that the gift of God may be purchased with money.

"Thou hast neither part nor lot in this matter: for thy heart is not right in the sight of God."

Outward show and hypocritical pretenses could not influence Peter any more than they could win the favor of God. Only a sincere heart was acceptable. Seeing that Simon's heart was set on making money at the sacrifice of honor, and even the desecration of the word of God, Peter told him to repent of his wickedness, and to pray to God for forgiveness, "for" he added, "I perceive that thou art in the gall of bitterness, and in the bond of iniquity."

Such a scathing rebuke, filled the sorcerer with fear, and he pleaded with Peter to pray to God "that none of these things which ye have spoken come upon me."

Peter continued for a short time to preach in other cities in Samaria and then returned to Jerusalem.

LESSON 15 AT LYDDA AND JOPPA

Church Established.

Though only a few years had passed since the Apostles had received the final commission to "Go into all the world and preach the Gospel," yet, through their earnest and continuous labors, churches were established in all Judea, Galilee and Samaria. As it was the duty of the Twelve to look after the interests of the whole Church, it became necessary for them to travel throughout all the land of the Jews. Peter visited from place to place, organizing, ordaining, blessing, and preaching the Gospel of Christ.

Eneas the Cripple.

On one of these tours, he visited the cities on the plain of Sharon, which border on the Mediterranean Sea. One of these towns was Lydda, in the southern part of the plain. While visiting the saints here, "he found a certain man named Eneas who had kept his bed eight years, and was sick of the palsy." This was a disease which affected the limbs of those afflicted, and made it impossible for them to walk. This poor cripple had not taken a step for eight years. Undoubtedly, he had heard that Christ had healed men as sorely afflicted as he, and also, that Peter, in the name of Christ, had bade the cripple at the Temple gate to arise and walk. At any rate, when Peter found him he appealed to Peter to give him the same blessing.

"And Peter said unto him, Eneas, Jesus Christ maketh thee whole: arise and make thy bed." This meant for him to fold the rug on which he was lying, and put away for the day. "He arose immediately. And all that dwelt at Lydda and Sharon saw him, and turned to the Lord."

Tabitha.

Not far distant from Lydda was another city named Joppa. One reason why we read of Joppa is because it was the home of a very good woman whom everybody loved. Her name in Hebrew was Tabitha, and in Greek was Dorcas. Both these words mean "Gazelle," the name of a very beautiful animal like a deer. Tabitha seems to have been as beautiful as she was good, and her whole time evidently was spent in giving comfort and happiness to others. She benefited the poor by presenting them with coats and garments that she made with her own hands. But one day she was taken sick, and all her many friends became very anxious about her. When her sickness grew worse and she died, all their hearts were filled with gloom. Among these sad mourners were some widows to whom Tabitha had given comfort. They were truly bowed in grief, as, indeed, was the entire Church at Joppa. After the body was tenderly washed, it was carried to an upper room.

But there was no funeral service held; for some of the disciples had heard that Peter was over at Lydda, and "They sent unto him two men, desiring him that he would not delay to come unto them."

Peter granted their request and went at once to Joppa. "When he was come, they brought him into the upper chamber: and all the widows stood by him weeping;" and, undoubtedly between their sobs, praising the virtues of their departed sister.

Following the example of his Master when the little daughter of Jairus was restored to life, Peter asked everybody in the room to leave. He then knelt down, and prayed. Turning toward the body, he said:

"Tabitha, arise."

Tabitha Restored.

As the first manifestation of life, we are told that "she opened her eyes." What her surprise upon seeing the Chief Apostle by her side instead of her nearer friends—what exchange of greetings were made—what expressions of gratitude, we cannot tell; but "he gave her his hand, and lifted her up, and when he had called the saints and widows, presented her alive."

As a result of this miracle, which became known throughout all Joppa, "many believed in the Lord."

Preached Only to Jews.

Up to this time the Apostles preached only to the Jews because being Jews themselves, they thought the Messiah was their Savior but not the Savior of other nations, especially of those nations who worshiped idols. All peoples nor Jews were called Gentiles and were considered by the Jews to be "common" or "unclean."

Cornelius.

Although the Lord had commanded to "teach all nations," yet the Apostles did not seem to have comprehended their commission, until Peter received a special vision.

While he was staying in Joppa with a man named Simon who was a tanner, there was a Roman officer stationed at Caesarea, thirty miles northward. His name was Cornelius. He was captain of a hundred soldiers, and was therefore called a "Centurion." Although a "Gentile," Cornelius did not worship idols as did most of the Gentiles.

A Devout Man.

Undoubtedly, he had heard of Christ, and knew that many of the Jews accepted Him as their Savior; and he wondered why the true Gospel could not save him as well as the Jews. "He was a devout man, and one that feared God" and taught all in his house to do likewise. Not only this, but he lived a righteous life, which is best of all, and gave also to the poor.

One afternoon, he was praying in his house when an angel appeared to him, and said, "Cornelius."

The suddenness of the angel's appearance filled the Centurion with fear; but he answered,

"What is it, Lord?"

His Prayers Answered.

"Thy prayers and thine alms are come up for a memorial before God," said the angel; "and now send men to Joppa, and call for one Simon, whose surname is Peter. He is staying with one Simon the tanner, whose house is by the seaside: he shall tell thee what thou oughtest to do."

As soon as the angel had gone, Cornelius called two servants and a soldier who also worshiped the Lord, and telling them what the angel had said, sent them to Joppa. They followed the seashore southward all night, and reached Joppa about noon the next day.

A Midday Vision.

Just about the hour that these messengers entered the city, Peter, as was his custom, went upon the housetop to pray. While there, waiting for the preparation of his noonday meal, he "fell into a trance," in which he saw coming down from heaven a vessel resembling "a great sheet knit at the four corners, and let down to earth, wherein were all manner of four-footed beasts, and creeping things, and fowls of the air."

While Peter beheld these animals, thinking they were unfit to eat, a voice said: "Rise, Peter; kill and eat."

"Not so, Lord; for I have never eaten anything that is common and unclean."

"What God hath cleansed," continued the voice, "that call not thou common."

This was repeated three times, and then the sheet was taken up again to heaven.

Peter Perplexed.

Peter was perplexed, and sat wondering what the vision might mean. However, he was not left long in doubt; for while he was thinking on the vision, "the Spirit said unto him, Behold three men seek thee. Arise, therefore, and get thee down, and go with them, doubting nothing: for I have sent them."

Now it happened that just while Peter was given his vision the three messengers from Cornelius knocked at Simon's door, and were admitted into his house. As Peter entered, and saw them, he said,

"Behold, I am he whom ye seek: what is the cause wherefore ye have come?"

"Cornelius, the centurion, * * * was warned from God by an holy angel," they answered, "to send for thee into his house, and to hear words of thee."

The messengers stayed that night with Peter in Simon's house; and next morning, conducted him and "certain brethren from Joppa," to Caesarea. On the following day, as they came to the Centurion's house, they found Cornelius and all his household, kinsmen, and friends gathered to receive them. As Peter neared the door, Cornelius stepped out to meet him, fell, down at his feet, and began to worship him. But Peter raised him up, saying gently:

"Stand up; I myself also am a man."

As the two men entered the house, Peter, seeing a number of people present, said:

Peter Communes With Gentiles.

"Ye know how that it is an unlawful thing for a man that is a Jew to keep company, or come unto one of another nation; but God hath showed me that I should not call any man common or unclean. * * * Now for what intent have ye sent for me?"

Cornelius then told all about his fasting and prayer, the visit of the angel, and the angel's instructions.[51]

The prejudice that had prevented Peter from comprehending the full meaning of the command to "Teach all nations," began to lift from his soul, his eyes began to see more clearly the mercy of our Heavenly Father; and as Cornelius ceased speaking, he exclaimed:

"Of a truth I perceive that God is no respecter of per sons: but in every nation he that feareth him, and worketh righteousness, is accepted with him."[52]

---

[51] See Acts 10:30-34

[52] See Acts 10:34-43

Then to this first meeting of Gentiles in the early Church, Peter told the story of the Redeemer, testifying of the Savior's death and resurrection.

Holy Ghost Given.

As final proof to the chief Apostles that the Lord would accept the Gentiles as well as the Jews into His Church, "the Holy Ghost fell on all them which heard the word."

Accepting this as a direct manifestation from God, Peter declared.

"Can any man forbid water, that these may be baptized, who have received the Holy Ghost as well as we?"

LESSON 16 THE THIRD IMPRISONMENT

"They never sought in vain that sought the Lord aright."
"If you cannot pray over a thing, and cannot ask God to bless you in it, don't do that thing. A secret that you would keep from God is a secret that you should keep from your own heart."

After having completed his labors at Lydda, Joppa, and the adjacent towns, Peter returned to Jerusalem and continued his earnest work in the ministry.

A Wicked King.

But there was a wicked king ruling over Judea at that time, named Herod Agrippa, who "stretched forth his hands to vex certain of the Church." He was a grandson of Herod the Great, who, you remember, slaughtered all the little children in Bethlehem in his effort to kill the little baby Jesus. He was also a nephew of Herod Antipas, the wicked king who had John the Baptist beheaded. Herod Agrippa possessed the same wicked passions as his grandfather and his uncle; so, of course, he hated and despised the righteous men who, in preaching the Gospel, were condemning sin and wickedness.

Peter Thrust Into Prison.

The first apostle to suffer from King Agrippa's wickedness was James the brother of John whom he killed "with the sword." When he found that this murderous act pleased the haughty and stiff-necked Jews, he thought he would kill some others of the apostolic band. Accordingly, he arrested Simon Peter; but, fortunately, concluded not to kill him until after Easter, so thrust him in prison until a more favorable time for a public execution.

Strongly Guarded.

As if to make sure that Peter would not escape this time, he "delivered him to four quarternions of soldiers to keep him." "This meant four distinct pickets of four guards each, sixteen in all. Each picket was to keep watch three hours and then be relieved by another during the night watches. Two officers must guard at the outer gate of the prison, and two be in the cell, one on each side of the prisoner, with his arms chained to them." Thus firmly guarded and chained, Peter lay down to sleep "between two soldiers, bound with two chains, and the keepers before the door."[53]

James' cruel death and the report of Peter's imprisonment spread consternation among the saints in Judea. Some, perhaps, were fearful; all were prayerful.

Special Assemblies in Prayer.

It seems that groups of earnest saints met in different places, and pleaded in sincere prayer to God to spare their leader's life. Indeed, "prayer was made without ceasing of the Church unto God for him." It is thought by some historians that among those who were thus supplicating the Lord were Paul and Barnabas who were probably in Jerusalem at that time.

At Mary's House.

One of the principal meetings was held at the house of Mary the mother of John Mark, who many years after, wrote the Gospel, according to St. Mark.

[53] Acts 12:6

ST. PETER IN PRISON.
"The angel of the Lord came upon him, and a light shined in the prison."

While we leave them in solemn prayer on the night before Peter was to be killed, let us go back to the prison, and see what is happening there.

An Angel Appears to Peter.

While Peter lay sleeping on his pallet of straw, "behold, the angel of the Lord came upon him, and a light shined in the prison." Evidently, the guards were asleep, and neither saw nor heard anything for the angel touched Peter on the side, and raised him up saying, "Arise up quickly."

As Peter complied, his chains fell off his hands. Then the angel said to him: "Tie your girdle around your waist, and put on your sandals."

Peter, scarcely knowing what he was doing, did as he was told. Then the angel continued:

"Cast thy garment about thee, and follow me."

Still thinking that he was dreaming, Peter followed the angel.

Peter Delivered From Prison.

They left the guards in the cell, passed the first guard of soldiers, then the second; but no one tried to stop them. When they came to the big "iron gate that leadeth to the city," it "opened to them of its own accord." The angel continued to direct Peter through one of the streets of the city, then left him as suddenly as he had appeared.

By this time, however, Peter fully realized that he was not dreaming, but was actually out of prison. He said to himself:

His Life Saved.

"Now I know of a surety, that the Lord hath sent his angel, and hath delivered me out of the hand of Herod, and from all the expectation of the Jews." By this last remark, he referred to the public execution that Herod had promised to have taken place that very day. But faith and prayers were more mighty in Peter's behalf than the decree of kings, and the demands of the wicked Jews.

Wondering just a little where he should go, he turned to the house of Mary, the mother of John Mark, where, you know, some of the saints were even at that moment praying for his deliverance.

Rhoda.

"As Peter knocked at the door of the gate," a young girl named Rhoda came, and asked who was there. When she heard Peter's voice, she was so glad that she didn't stop to open the gate, but ran immediately into the room saying:

"Peter is here—standing outside the door."

Friends Astonished.

So suddenly interrupted in their prayer, the people would not believe her, but said she was beside herself. But Rhoda insisted that she was right. She knew Peter's voice, and she knew he was at the door. They finally concluded that "it was his angel."

In the meantime, Peter kept knocking until he was finally admitted. It seems that the little group hardly expected their prayers to be answered in just that literal way; so "when they opened the door and saw him, they were astonished."

Peter, holding up his hand, and beckoning them to be quiet, told them how the Lord had delivered him from prison. Then he added: "Go explain all these things to James, and to the brethren." This James was probably the brother of Jesus, who seems to have been appointed to take charge of the Church at Jerusalem.[54]

Peter Gets Away.

Knowing that as soon as he would be missed in prison the soldiers of old Herod would be searching for him, Peter went unto another place.

When morning came, there was a great stir among the soldiers because of Peter's having escaped. Herod ordered a thorough search in vain.

Then, thinking the keepers of the prison had been careless and negligent, this wicked ruler ordered them put to death.

Guards Put to Death.

Not long afterward he, himself, died so suddenly and so miserably, that some said the wrath of God was visited upon him because of his wickedness. Luke tells us that the "angel of the Lord smote him."

Herod's Death.

But Peter, whom Herod had sought to kill, was spared, through the blessings of the Lord, to bless the Church, and to preach the Gospel for many years afterward.

---

[54] Gal. 1:19

LESSON 17 CLOSING SCENES OF A RIGHTEOUS MINISTRY

"The Gospel is the fulfillment of all hopes, the perfection of all philosophy, the interpreter of all revelations, and a key to all the seeming contradictions of truth in the physical and moral world."

Peter's Character.

Many years have passed since Peter met Jesus, and was told that he should be called "Cephas which is by interpretation, a Stone." Little did Peter realize then, why the Lord desired to have this fisherman's character become as a rock. Little did he realize what mighty responsibility his Master desired to place upon him. But the years that have intervened have been filled with wonderful experiences, all of which tended to make Peter not only the Rock-man Christ had desired him to become, but the great leader and chief apostle in the Church of Christ.

Fearlessness, faithfulness, prayerfulness, humility, and an untiring zeal in his efforts to instruct and to bless the people are traits of Peter's character that shine out in his life.

We should be reminded, however, that this rock character was not formed all at once. It grew gradually. You remember how Jesus, watching its formation, reproved Peter's weaknesses, commended his strength, and encouraged him, time after time, to remain true to the work as a "fisher of men."

A "Fisher of Men."

We have now reached that period in his life when this man who at one time pulled nets full of fishes from the sea of Galilee can look back over his years of ministry and see numberless nets full of men, women, and children drawn from the sea of ignorance and sin and put safely in the Church of Christ.

There was this difference, however, between the results of his fishing for fish and his fishing for men: The fish he dragged from the element of life to physical death; the men he drew from the element of death to eternal life.

For five years after his deliverance from the third imprisonment, Peter continued his visits from city to city, province to province, preaching the Word of the Lord. During many of these travels, he was, undoubtedly, accompanied by his faithful wife.

Opened Door to Gentiles.

It had been Peter's duty and privilege to preach the Gospel first to the Gentiles. Please note that when the Lord desired the Gentiles to hear His word, He instructed the Chief of the Twelve to turn the key that opened the Gospel door to them. This is one of the special duties of the Apostleship.

Christians.

Since that time, many Gentiles had become converted; and in some cities they met and worshiped together with the Jews. This was particularly true in Antioch, an important city of Syria where the followers of Jesus were first called Christians.

But there were certain men from Judea who went to Antioch and caused trouble. These were Jews who had accepted the Gospel, but who still believed that the Gentiles would have to do everything the Jews did before they could obtain salvation.

Peter Justifies the Gentiles.

The question as to whether the Gentiles might receive the Gospel and be saved, without conforming to every Jewish rite, came before the Twelve and other Church leaders in Jerusalem.

"And when there had been much disputing, Peter arose up, and said unto them:

"Men and brethren, ye know how that a good while ago God made choice among us, that the Gentiles by my mouth should hear the work of the Gospel and believe.

"And God, who knoweth the hearts, bare them witness, giving them the Holy Ghost, even as he did unto us;

"And put no difference between us and them, purifying their hearts by faith."

He then told them not to provoke God by passing some rule that would compel the Gentiles to do what the Lord does not require of them. For, he added, "We believe that through the grace of the Lord Jesus Christ, we shall be saved, even as they."

Upholds the Right.

There was a time when Simon, the Jewish fisherman, with all his Jewish prejudices, would have rather yielded to the Jewish side of this question; but now, it was not Simon, the fisherman, who spoke, but Peter, the chief apostle of the Lord. What were prejudices to him in the light of the inspiration of truth! All that was necessary for him to know was, whether the thing was right, and prejudice or no prejudice, favor or no favor, he would defend it.

It is true that once after this council, so Paul says.[55] Peter withdrew from the company of some Gentiles because some of the Jews came down from Jerusalem. Paul says he rebuked Peter for his actions on this occasion; but we have no record of what Peter said or did. Knowing Peter as we do, we are safe in concluding that he did not intentionally waver from the right. It seems more probable that Paul misunderstood Peter's motives. At any rate, we may rest assured that what Peter said and did was intended to help those who were influenced by his actions.

Visits All Churches.

From that time, we know very little of Peter's travels. By reading his epistles, we get a little insight into the nature of his labors and travels during the last years of his life. Undoubtedly, he visited every country where there were organized branches of the Church, even to the "seven churches in Asia."

Thirty-five Years' Service.

We do not know just where he died, nor the kind of death he suffered; but it is evident that the end was not far off when he wrote his second epistle to the churches. That was about thirty-five years after he first met the Savior. He was in the ministry then, approximately thirty-five years, perhaps longer.

Referring to the prophecy of the Lord on the shore of Galilee, the aged apostle, writing to the Saints and urging them to be true to the Gospel, said:

"Knowing that shortly I must put off this my tabernacle, even as our Lord Jesus Christ hath showed me. Moreover, I will endeavor that ye may be able after my decease to have these things always in remembrance."

Some of the earliest Christian writers tell us that Peter and Paul were both imprisoned in Rome during the terrible persecutions of the Saints under the wicked King Nero.

A Legend.

There is a story told that before Nero had imprisoned Peter, the Saints, perceiving the danger he was in, pleaded with him to leave Rome.

Very reluctantly, he yielded to their entreaties, and escaped from the city, by night. As he was going away, he met the Lord carrying

---

[55] Gal. 2:7

His cross, and going toward Rome. "Master, whither art thou going?" asked Peter. "To Rome, to be crucified a second time," was the reply.

Thinking that if his Lord could be crucified a second time for the Truth, he too, would be willing to die for in, he returned to Rome, and some time later, was condemned by the Emperor Nero to suffer death by crucifixion. As he neared the place of execution, however, Peter asked that he be permitted to hang on the cross with his head downwards, which request was granted.

These circumstances are more or less legendary, and may or may not be true; but this we know that whatever the manner or time of his death Simon Peter died true to every trust that his Lord and Master had given him

"He has done the work of a true man,—
Crown him, honor him, love him.
Weep over him, tears of woman,
Stoop manliest brows above him!
No duty could overtake him,
No need his will outrun;
Or ever our lips could ask him.
His hands the work had done."

PART TWO—JAMES
LESSON 18 JAMES, THE SON OF ZEBEDEE

"Honor and shame from no condition rise;
Act well thy part, there all the honor lies."
"Honor is not a matter of any man's calling merely; but rather of his own actions in it."

Among the devoted women who followed Jesus in Galilee, who ministered unto Him, and watched with anxious care and sorrow the progress of the trials in Jerusalem, was a noble mother named Salome. With Mary Magdalene, and Mary the mother of Jesus and Joses, she stood "beholding afar off" the crucifixion of the Savior.

She was one who would not forsake her Lord even at the cross. She was also one who, with spices and perfumes, went early to the sepulchre Sunday morning, to participate in the embalming of Jesus' body. To her and others, the Savior appeared, that morning, saying, "Be not afraid; go tell my brethren that they go into Galilee, and there shall they see me."

Tennyson Quoted.

"Happy he with such a mother! faith in womankind beats with his blood, and trust in all things high comes easy to him, and though he trip and fall, he shall not blind his soul with clay."

Proud of Her Boys.

Such was the faithful, devoted woman whom James and John, the sons of Zebedee called mother. And she was as proud of her boys as they were proud of their mother; for they seemed to have inherited from their mother, and perhaps their father too, those true and unwavering qualities which made them such devoted disciples of Christ.

A Mother's Request.

Like most mothers, Salome desired to see her boys honored; and one day asked the Savior to grant that her two sons might sit, the one on His right hand the other on the left, in His kingdom. Jesus said, "Are ye able to drink of the cup that I shall drink of, and be baptized with the baptism that I am baptized with?"

They answered, "We are able."

Boys to Drink of Cup.

"Ye shall drink indeed of my cup, and be baptized with the baptism that I am baptized with," answered the Lord; "but to sit on my right hand, and on my left, is not mine to give."

True Servants.

The mother's eagerness to have her sons thus honored made the other ten a little jealous; but when Jesus saw their feelings, He told them that while men who hold offices in the world exercise unrighteous dominion, those who are given offices in His Church are the servants of all. "Whosoever will be chief among you let him be your servant."

Of Bethsaida.

James was of Bethsaida, in Galilee, and was a fisherman. He was busy at his trade when Jesus called him to the ministry. When the call came, James and his brother were sitting in a boat mending nets. Their father and hired servants were also there. Of course, James had seen Jesus before this, and had undoubtedly heard Him; for when Andrew had hurried off to find Simon Peter, after having met the Lord, John had hurried to find his brother James.

Accepts Call.

So James, too, had found the Messiah, and was already converted to the Gospel. Therefore when Jesus stopped that morning by the seashore, and said, "Come, I will make you fishers of men," they immediately left their father with the hired servants, and followed Christ.

One of the Twelve.

When the Twelve were chosen, James was chosen next to Peter, and was one of the three who constituted what we might call the Presidency of the Twelve. In this position, he became closely associated with the Redeemer, and was an eyewitness to some of the most sacred incidents in His Lord's ministry. Thus, with Peter and John, he was present in the room when the little daughter of Jairus was restored to life.

On the Mount.

He was also one of the favored three on the Mount of Transfiguration; and was one of those chosen to accompany the Master to the secluded place in the Garden of Gethsemane, when

Christ suffered those bitter agonies preparatory to His betrayal and sufferings on the cross.

A Son of Thunder.

James was called a son of Thunder; and there is one incident in the Bible which gives us a little insight into a part of his nature which probably called forth that name. When the time came that Jesus was determined to go to Jerusalem to be offered up as a sacrifice, he "sent messengers before His face: and they went, and entered into a village of the Samaritans, to make ready for him."[56]

James was one of these messengers.

But the Samaritans, who would have no dealings with the Jews, and who were particularly offended on this occasion because Jesus was determined to worship in Jerusalem, refused to receive Jesus. Their refusal made James and John so indignant that they turned to their Master and said: "Lord let us command fire to come down from heaven, and consume them, even as Elias did?"

A Rebuke.

But the Lord was displeased with them for being angry, and said, "Ye know not what manner of spirit ye are of. For the Son of Man is not come to destroy men's lives but to save them."

For this almost righteous manifestation of fire in their natures, it is thought that James and John were called Boanerges, or "sons of Thunder."

Little Recorded of His Labors.

But if he had an impetuous nature or quick temper, he controlled it, and through his faithfulness and devotion won the favor of his Lord.

It is thought that he traveled a great deal, preaching the Gospel, it is said, to all the dispersed tribes of Israel. But of his labors, there is scarcely any record.

The First Martyr.

About forty-two or forty-four years after Christ, Herod Agrippa, as you have already learned, commenced a bitter persecution against the Saints. James was among the first to be arrested.

Officer Converted.

---

[56] Luke 9:52

Sentence was passed upon him very soon after he was apprehended, yet, so remarkable were his faith and his courage during the trial that the officer who guarded him, (who, some say, was his accuser) repented of his sins, became converted, and declared his faith in Christianity.

As James was being led to the place of execution, this officer threw himself at the apostle's feet, and humbly begged forgiveness for what he had said against him.

Putting his arm around the penitent man, James answered, "Peace, my son, peace be unto thee, and pardon of thy faults."

Execution.

Both were then executed by order of the cruel Herod. Thus James, the first martyr apostle, partook of the cup of which he had said to his Lord many years before he was willing to drink.

PART THREE—JOHN
LESSON 19 WITH THE REDEEMER

"Modesty is a shining light; it prepares the mind to receive knowledge, and the heart for truth."
"Humility is the solid foundation of all the virtues."

Modesty.

In the first chapter of the Gospel according to St. John, we read that two disciples of John the Baptist heard their master bear witness to the divinity of Jesus. Said the Baptist, referring to Jesus walking alone in the distance, "Behold the Lamb of God, that taketh away the sin of the world." One of the two disciples who heard this testimony is named; he was Andrew, the brother of Simon Peter.[57] The other is not named. Indeed throughout the entire book, which undoubtedly, was written by St. John, himself, the name of John, son of Zebedee, is never once written. In the account of the Last Supper, we read of a "disciple whom Jesus loved," who sat so near the Lord that his head could rest on Jesus' bosom.

These two instances, and others that might be named indicate to us a prominent trait in St. John's character; viz., an unassumed modesty that won him the respect and love of all who knew him.

Fearlessness.

But John was the son of Salome and Zebedee, and the younger brother of James, with whim he was called "Boanerges," or son of Thunder. This gives us a little insight into another phase of his character. Like his brother James, he was evidently fiery in his zeal in whatever he undertook to do, and fearless in doing what he thought was right.

57 John 1:40

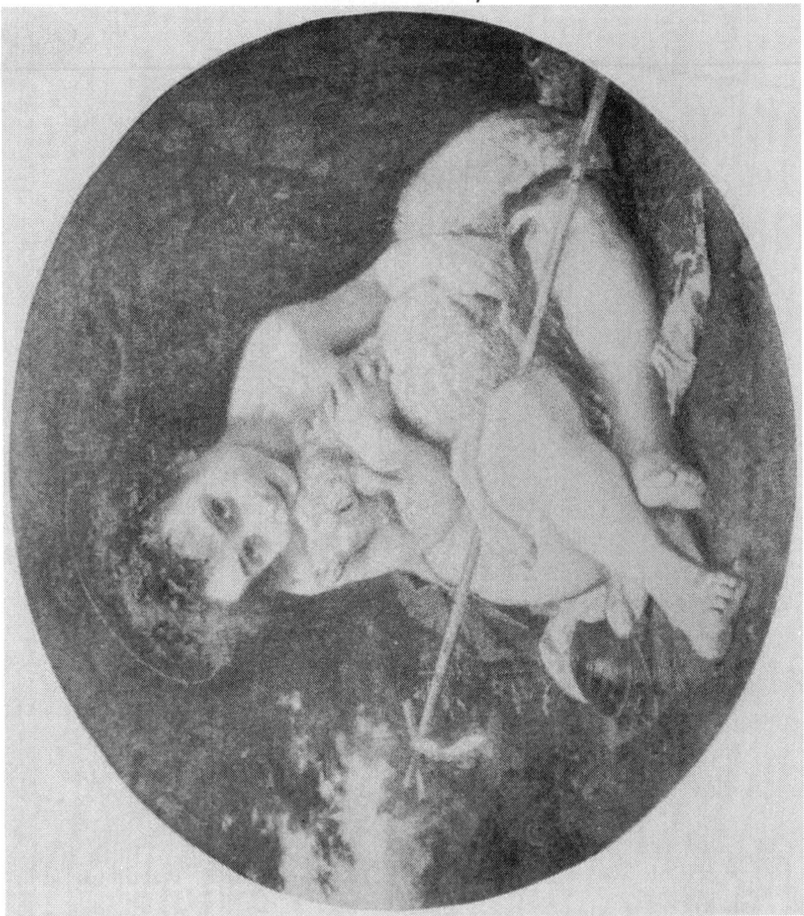

ST. JOHN AND THE LAMB.

Love.

A modesty that made him shrink ever from praising himself or unduly pushing himself forward; a *fearlessness* in defending what is right, and a *love* for his Master that gave him the highest place in the Savior's heart—these are three traits of John's character which stand out distinctly in the fragmentary accounts of his life.

He lived, and was probably born in Bethsaida, the home of Peter and Andrew and Philip. He was a fisherman by trade, and worked with his father and brother James. His father, Zebedee, owned his own ships, and employed servants; so we conclude that he was well to do financially.[58]

A Seeker After Truth.

[58] Mark 1:20

He was a seeker after true learning, and especially after those things which would tell him about God and the hereafter. He kept his mind and heart pure, so that he could appreciate the truth when he heard it.

When, therefore, John the Baptist came out of the wilderness preaching repentance and declaring that the "Kingdom of Heaven was at hand," John was one of the fearless young men who believed the Baptist and followed him. Thus he was prepared to accept John's testimony of Jesus after the latter was baptized in Jordan, and was one of the two who had the first interview with the Savior of the world at the beginning of His ministry.

Follows Jesus.

On the same occasion when Simon Peter and his brother were called as disciples of Jesus, "James the son of Zebedee and John were with their father mending their nets," and when Jesus called them, they immediately left the ship and their father and followed Him.[59]

A First Lesson.

Luke tells us[60] that John was present at the miraculous draught of fishes, and was very much astonished at what he heard and saw on that occasion. It was one of the first lessons if not the first impressive lesson that taught him the great truth that obedience to Christ's words bring blessings.

Youngest of the Twelve.

From this time on to the end of his eventful life, he was always in the ministry. When Jesus chose his disciples, John was chosen one of the special three, although he was the youngest member of the Twelve.

Memorable Experiences.

From that time, John was in the close companionship of Jesus, and witnessed some of the most remarkable and divine incidents recorded in the history of Christ's ministry. He was one of the three apostles permitted to remain in the room when the little daughter of Jairus was restored to life.[61] He was on the mount of Transfiguration when the Savior conversed with Moses and Elias and when a voice from heaven said "This is my beloved Son, hear him."[62]

---

[59] Matt. 4:21, 22; Luke 5:1-11

[60] Luke 5:1-11

[61] Luke 8:51

[62] Luke 9:28

With Peter, James and Andrew, John was present on the Mount of Olives when Jesus taught them concerning the destrucion of the temple, and of Christ's second coming. How the memory of such occasions must have filled his soul in after years, with rejoicing and sweet content!

To him and Peter was entrusted the duty of making preparations for the Passover.[63]

Close to Jesus.

At the solemn moment when the Savior said "One of you shall betray me," it was John the "disciple whom Jesus loved" who received the answer indicating who the traitor was.

In Gethsemane.

When the gloom of Gethsemane began to weigh heavily upon the spirit of Jesus, John was one of the three unto whom He said, "My soul is exceeding sorrowful unto death; tarry ye here and watch."[64]

In the House of the High Priest.

Later that same night, when the traitor gave the kiss of betrayal, and the soldiers arrested Jesus, and bore Him away a prisoner, all the other disciples fled, but John accompanied his Master to the house of the high priest and later admitted Peter, who, you remember, had "followed afar off."

A Terrible Ordeal.

Though we are not told, yet we can imagine what this beloved disciple's feelings were as he listened to the false and wicked accusations against his Lord, and how his heart must have ached as he saw Jesus beaten and scourged, and a crown of thorns put on His head. If he had wanted to call down fire from heaven and consume the Samaritans who refused shelter and accommodations to his Lord, what must have been the state of his fiery soul when he beheld the Jews and their judges persecuting the Christ to death!

A Last Request.

How his soul must have been rent in agony as he saw his Savior nailed to the cross, and yet what peace must have come to him as he received from the dying lips of his Master one of the dearest commissions ever given to mortal man! As the three Marys and John

---

[63] Luke 22:8
[64] Mark 14:33

stood by the cross, Jesus looked down upon them and said to his mother, "Woman, behold thy Son!" and to John, "Behold thy mother!"

"And from that hour that disciple took her unto his own home."

On the Sunday morning following the crucifixion, John was with Peter when Mary Magdalene came running to them, saying:

At the Tomb.

"They have taken away the Lord out of the sepulchre, and we know not where they have laid Him."

As soon as the apostles heard this, they ran for the spot where Jesus had been buried. John being the younger outran Peter and was the first to see the empty tomb; and "looking in, saw the linen clothes lying, yet went he not in." A moment later, however, he followed Peter into the tomb, made a careful examination of the linen clothes and napkin that was about the head; but not yet realizing that Christ was to rise the third day, each returned to his own home.

His Testimony.

John was with the ten and later with the Eleven when Christ appeared to them in the upper room. Of this and other glorious experiences he bears testimony in his Gospel. "That ye might believe in Jesus Christ, the Son of God, and that believing ye might have life through His name."

LESSON 20 WITH PETER AND THE TWELVE

"Love one human being purely and warmly and you will love all."
"Love gives itself, it is not bought."

At the Sea of Galilee.

John was one of those who, after the death and resurrection of Jesus, when Simon Peter said, "I go a fishing" replied: "We also go with you." They toiled all night, and caught nothing, but when morning came they were told by a man on the shore to "Cast the net on the right side of the ship." This they did and caught a multitude of fishes. Almost immediately John recognized Jesus and said to Peter, "It is the Lord."

Feed My Sheep.

A little later, on the shore, he heard the Savior's admonition to Peter to feed the sheep and the lambs in the fold of Christ, and no doubt John shared in the feeling of responsibility that was then thrown upon the Twelve.

It was on this occasion that Peter asked Jesus what would become of John, to which question Jesus made the significant reply, "If I will that he tarry till I come, what is that to thee? follow thou me."

A Prophecy.

"Then went this saying abroad among the brethren that that disciple should not die: yet Jesus said not unto him, He shall not die; but if I will that he tarry till I come, what is that to thee?"

In this connection we read in the Doctrine and Covenants[65] that John had said to the Lord, "Give me power over death that I may live and bring souls unto Thee."

And the Lord answered, "Verily, verily, I say unto thee, because thou desired this, thou shalt tarry until I come in my glory, and shalt prophesy before nations, kindred, tongues and people."

The Lord then told Peter that He would make John "as a flaming fire and a ministering angel; he shall minister for those who shall be heirs of salvation who dwell on the earth."

True Greatness.

---

[65] Section 7

Thus was expressed John's love not only for his Lord and Master but for all the children of men whom he desired to bring to Christ and to participate in the joys of the everlasting gospel. By this spirit, John proved himself to have been one of the greatest men that ever lived; for true greatness consists in losing oneself for the good of others.

True to Trust.

For about fifteen years after the Savior's ascension it is believed that John continued at Jerusalem and remained a true son to the Virgin Mary. During all that time, however, he was always active in the ministry.

The Impotent Man.

He was with Peter going to the temple when the lame men at the gate Beautiful asked them for alms. With Peter he exercised His faith on that occasion to bless the poor man who had never walked.[66]

The Impotent Man.

John, undoubtedly, testified to the multitude who assembled at Solomon's porch on the day of this miracle; but no historian has told us what he said. We infer from what Luke says that John spoke at that time; but only Peter's sermon and only a little of that has been preserved.

While they were speaking the captain of the temple arrested them and put them in prison.

Before the Council.

When they were brought out before the Council next day and told not to preach about Jesus any more, John was just as bold as Peter in declaring, "Whether it be right in the sight of God to hearken unto you more than God, judge ye, for we cannot but speak the things which we have seen and heard."[67]

Spiritual Minded.

After they were released, they continued preaching to the people and praising the Lord for all His wonderful manifestations to them. The great spiritual feast that resulted from their labors must have filled John's soul with a divine peace such as he had never before experienced, for of all the apostles, he was the most spiritual minded.

---

[66] Relate the incident. Acts 3:1-12

[67] Acts 4:19-20

A True Servant.

During this period, he was imprisoned several times, but never once did he waver in his determination to let all the people know that Jesus Christ was the Redeemer of the World. He could suffer and be happy because he loved those whom he served. Thus in the beginning of his ministry his character shone out in true greatness; for he was "willing, patient and strong to endure for others."

In Samaria.

When the Samaritans received the Gospel through the preaching of Philip, John accompanied Peter to Samaria, and conferred the Holy Ghost by the laying on of hands, upon those whom Philip had baptized.[68]

Various Officers.

No doubt this was just one of many such visits he made during those fifteen years that he remained at Jerusalem. The Twelve, the seventies, elders, priests, teachers and deacons were out preaching in all the cities round about Jerusalem, and the three chief Apostles, Peter, James and John would be required, and when not required would be invited, to organize the branches and to meet with the new converts and give encouragement in their glorious faith.

Pillar of the Church.

When the great question arose about what the Gentiles who joined the church should be required to do, John was one who sat in the council held at Jerusalem. Paul, writing about this council, mentions James, Cephas and John who "seemed to be pillars." In the light of the organization of the Church today, we know that Peter, James, and John were the men who presided at that time, although it was James who rendered the decision that was made effective throughout all the provinces.

Heart Filled With Love.

After that time, we know very little of John's ministry. Part of what is known will be given in the next lesson. We learn more about what kind of man he was than about what he did. When we read his letters to the church and his Gospel, we can readily understand why Jesus chose him to take care of His mother Mary. John's heart was full of love, and he wanted everybody to love everybody else. He said that anybody who "saith he is in the light, and hateth his brother is in

---

[68] Acts 8:5-14

darkness even until now. He that loveth his brother abideth in the light.

"But he that hateth his brother is in darkness and knoweth not whither he goeth, because that darkness hath blinded his eyes.

"I write unto you, little children, because your sins are forgiven you for His name's sake." In that same letter he says, "And now, little children, abide in Christ, that when He shall appear, we may have confidence and not be ashamed before Him and His coming."

LESSON 21 CLOSING SCENES OF MINISTRY

"Love was to his impassioned soul, not a mere part of its existence, but the whole, the very life-breath of his heart."

Eighteen Years Pass.

The important council mentioned in the last chapter was held about 50 years after the birth of Christ (50 A. D.) During the next eighteen years John seems to have been hidden from view. Nothing is known about what he did or where he went. It is presumed that he left Jerusalem, and seldom, if ever, returned. If so, then we may rightly conclude that Mary the mother of Jesus had left Jerusalem also, and left it and all her loving kindred and friends on earth for a happy, glorious meeting with her Son in their heavenly home on high. The dutiful and loving attention John had bestowed upon Mary, he is now free to give to the Church which now bears her Son's name.

Undoubtedly he visited nearly all, if not all the important places where Christians dwelt; but most of his latest years seem to have been spent in Asia Minor.

At Ephesus.

Tradition informs us that he made his home at Ephesus, a large and populous city of Iona about 40 miles from Smyrna. It was noted chiefly for its wickedness and the beautiful temple of Diana. Some claim that the Virgin Mary and Mary Magdalene went to Ephesus with John and died there. The tradition is a pleasing one; for with the devotion of a son to his mother, as shown by John, there is associated Mary Magdalene's love, which might well be expressed in the words of another beautiful woman, who said to her husband's mother, "Intreat me not to leave thee or to return from following after thee: for whither thou goest, I will go; and where thou lodgest, I will lodge; thy people shall be my people, and thy God my God; Where thou diest, will I die, and there will I be buried."[69]

From Ephesus John visited all the branches of the Church, laboring especially among "The Seven Churches in Asia."

When John had spent several years at Ephesus a cruel Roman emperor, during his persecution of the Church, arrested him, had him carried to Rome, condemned him to death, and had him plunged into boiling oil. John's life being preserved through the power of God, he was then banished to Patmos. All that John says about it is that he was

---

[69] Ruth 1:16, 17

"in the isle that is called Patmos, for the Word of God, and for the testimony of Jesus Christ." It is quite evident from this that he had been persecuted for his belief in the Gospel and for his unwavering testimony of the life, death and resurrection of Jesus Christ. He was probably the last living witness of the Savior's miracles and teachings. Perhaps that is why he was banished. But wicked men could not banish the testimony he had borne. That was planted in the hearts of thousands of sincere believers, and like seeds sown in fertile soil, would grow and bear rich harvests for ages to come.

Nor did banishment injure the aged apostle, for he was not alone even on that uninhabited and barren rock. One Sunday morning, on the "Lord's Day" as he called it, he "heard behind him a great voice, as of a trumpet" that said to him, "What thou seest write in a book and send it unto the seven churches which are in Asia." He turned, and saw the Son of Man clothed with a garment down to the foot, and bound with a golden girdle. As he beheld his Lord wrapped in such divine splendor, "he fell at His feet as dead." But the Savior, John says, "laid His right hand upon me, saying unto me. Fear not, I am the First and the Last, I am He that liveth, and was dead, and behold I am alive forever more." He was again commanded to write all he had witnessed and what would yet be shown him in vision. Thus was given to the seven churches of Asia, and subsequently to the world, what is now known as "Revelation," the last book in the Bible, but the first one written by its author.

Upon the death of Domitian, the cruel emperor who had banished him, the Apostle was permitted to return to Ephesus, where he continued his preaching, writing, and testimony.

John's Writings.

Besides "Revelation," he wrote his Gospel and his three Epistles.

John's second Epistle should be of special interest to the young. From it we infer that there were two Christian homes, in each of which John took delight. The mothers were sisters. His letter is addressed to "The Elect Lady" or, as she is sometimes called, the Lady Electa and her children. John tells of his love and that of others for them—mother and children—because of their Christian character. He tells of his great joy because of the children walking in the truth, living as children should live who have learned of the teachings of Christ.

ST. JOHN.
The Apostle and Evangelist.

It is said that when he became so old and feeble that he could not walk to church, nor preach to his people, his loving friends would carry him to the place of meeting. On these occasions, he would repeat again and again, "My dear children, love one another." One day some asked him, "Master, why dost thou always say this?" He answered. "This is what the Lord commands you; and this, if you do it, is sufficient."

It is said that he lived to be over one hundred years of age, but of his last days there is nothing definite of record. We do know, however, that he survived most bitter persecution, outlived his wicked persecutors, instructed by his life and teachings thousands in the Way of life, and is blessing many thousands in the world today, by his lofty and childlike Christian spirit.

"Beloved, follow not that which is evil, but that which is good. He that doeth good is of God, but he that doeth evil hath not seen God."

PART FOUR—PAUL AND HIS COMPANIONS.
LESSON 22 SAUL OF TARSUS

"Good company, and good discourses are the very sinews of virtue."

A Benjaminite.

At the time that Peter and Andrew, James and John were boys playing in Bethsaida, on the shores of Galilee, there was another bright, clever little lad playing and studying in a town about three hundred miles from them, whom they were to know in after years, first as a bitter enemy and afterwards as a friend and brother. This boy's name was Saul, and he lived in Tarsus, the capital of Cilicia. He was a Jew and belonged to the tribe of Benjamin, the youngest son of Jacob. Benjamin's father, you remember, kept him home when the other sons first went to Egypt to buy corn. The tribe of Benjamin was said to have been valorous; and in this respect, you will see that Saul was a true Benjaminite.

Other Members of Family.

Of Saul's parents and boyhood days we know very little. His father, at one time, lived in Palestine, and would, of course, teach his son to be a good orthodox Jew. Of his mother we know nothing, but we may be sure that she watched over him carefully, guided him in his games and in his studies and inspired him, even in his youth, to desire to grow up to be a great and useful man. Undoubtedly, this was the kind of mother he had, for all great men have been blest with just such noble mothers. We are not told whether he had any brothers; but he had at least one sister, whom he always loved and to whom he was a true and noble brother all his life.

A Good student.

Saul was a good student, and attended school probably from the time he was six years old until he became a man. But in those days, school boys had no school books. They would just listen to what their teacher told them, remember it, and try to be able to tell it again when asked to do so. The principal study in the schoolroom, at that time, was the holy scriptures. Of course, they did not have the Bible then as we have it now, but they had the Old Testament, and could learn all about Abraham, Isaac, and Jacob, the children of Israel. King Saul, King David, King Solomon and the prophets. Thus, he was taught early in his life to look forward to the Messiah who should be King of the Jews.

Pharisees and Sadducees.

Among the Jews were found different sects or religions, chief among which were the Pharisees and the Sadducees. In Saul's day, Pharisees were the most popular of all the sects, and held most of the highest offices in the state and the church. They believed in the oral law as delivered from God to Moses, as well as in the written law. They believed also in the resurrection of the body. But they made long and frequent prayers, not only in the synagogue and temple, but in the streets, so they could be heard of men. In other things, too, they were very hypocritical.

The Sadducees did not believe in a bodily resurrection. You will see, later, how Saul used to good advantage this difference of belief between these two sects.

A Pharisee.

Saul was a Pharisee; and a good Pharisee, too. He was just as sincere in his belief and education as any good man could be. If Saul had been a hypocritical Pharisee, he probably never would have found the truth, but being sincere, that is, always doing what he thought was right, he was led to the Gospel.

A Roman Citizen.

There is another thing to learn about this boy, "Saul of Tarsus;" viz., that he was born a Roman citizen. Tarsus, an exceedingly rich and populous city, was a Roman municipium, or free corporation. This means that the freedom of Rome (which ruled all those countries at that time) had been given to the freemen of Tarsus. This freedom had been granted because the men of Tarsus had defended two emperors of Rome during a rebellion against them.

Thus, Saul, though a Jew, was a freeborn Roman citizen. In this double capacity, he had two names, Saul and Paul; the first his Jewish name and the latter his Roman or Latin name.

A Tentmaker.

As has been said, Saul was a student; but he was industrious, not only with his head, but also with his hands. He was a tentmaker. This trade he learned when he was still a boy. It was a constant practice of the Jews to bring their children to some honest calling that, in case of necessity, they might provide for themselves by the labor of their own hands. The time came when Paul, though an apostle, labored at intervals for twenty-nine years at the trade his father had taught him. It was during such times that he wrote "These hands have ministered unto my necessities."

Gamaliel.

When Saul had completed the studies as given in the Jewish schools at Tarsus, and had learned his trade, he desired to attend college. He was then, probably, about fourteen years of age. There were Gentile universities near his home, but, as he wanted to become a Rabbi, he went to Jerusalem, and became a student in the famous "School of Hillel." The president of this noted institution of learning was, "a Pharisee named Gamaliel, a doctor of the law had in reputation among all the people."[70] It is supposed that he was a son of Simeon who was in the Temple when the little baby Jesus was blessed, and who said, "Lord, now lettest Thou Thy servant depart in peace; for mine eyes have seen Thy salvation."

But though Gamaliel was the most learned man of his day, he did not know that the Messiah had come. Evidently, he did not believe what his father had told him about the child Jesus.

Under the instruction and influence of his great teacher, Saul continued for several years studying in Hebrew and Greek, and memorizing all the important commandments which the old Testament contained.

Stephen.

Saul completed his course under Gamaliel, and probably returned to Cilicia. In the meantime, Jesus had been crucified and a bitter persecution against some of His disciples had begun. The first to suffer death during this persecution was Stephen, one of the seven deacons chosen to look after the funds for the poor. Stephen was a very faithful servant "full of faith and the Holy Ghost." He declared that Jesus was the Savior of the world, and that all men must believe in His name if they would be saved. Stephen knew that the Pharisees were wrong in what they thought was necessary to salvation, and he, undoubtedly, told them so. At any rate he disputed with them in the synagogue.

Stephen Before Sanhedrin.

Being defeated in their disputations, the angry Jews dragged Stephen before the Sanhedrin and accused him of blasphemy. Even in court he still bore testimony of the divinity, death and persecution of

---

[70] Acts 5:34

the Savior, which so maddened the wicked Jews that they "gnashed on him with their teeth," and finally dragged him out of the court room, and stoned him to death.

Consents to Stephen's Death.

Among those blinded Pharisees who disputed with Stephen, was the young, learned student, Saul of Tarsus. And when "they cried out with a loud voice, and stopped their ears, and ran upon him with one accord," Saul consented unto his death, held the cloaks of the murderers and stood by and witnessed the cruel death of this first Christian martyr. Saul was sincere in believing that Stephen was an enemy to the Jewish religion. Probably Stephen recognized this when, just as he was dying he prayed, "Lord, lay not this sin to their charge."

ST. PAUL.

LESSON 23 SAUL'S CONVERSION

"Better is the wrong with sincerity, rather than the right with falsehood."

A Bitter Persecutor.

His Sincerity.

After the death of Stephen, "there was a great persecution against the church which was at Jerusalem; and they were all scattered abroad, throughout the regions of Judea and Samaria." One of the Saints' most energetic and persistent persecutors, during those terrible days, was the blinded Pharisee, Saul, of Tarsus. So determined was he to put an end to what he thought was a heresy that he secured the right as an officer of the Sanhedrin to arrest the followers of Jesus wherever he found them. He went from house to house, dragging men from their wives and children. He even arrested the women, and thrust them in prison! Surely the cries and piteous pleadings of the little children must have rent even his bitter heart almost more than the martyrdom of the faithful Stephen. Surely, as he forced men and women away from their homes, the blanched faces of crouching children, and their heartbroken sobs must have imprinted upon his bigoted soul impressions that would humble him if not haunt him all the days of his life! Only one thing could give him comfort in later life as he looked back upon those awful experiences. It was this, as expressed in his own words: "I verily thought with myself that I ought to do many things contrary to the name of Jesus of Nazareth." Saul was sincere in what he was doing. He did not believe that Jesus Christ was the Son of God, and thought it would be pleasing to his Father in Heaven to make every believer in Christ deny His name.

Made Havoc of the Church.

So Saul "made havoc of the church;" and when he had either imprisoned or driven out of Jerusalem every man he could find who confessed the Christ, with his soul "yet breathing out threatenings and slaughter against the disciples of the Lord," he asked the High Priest for "letters to Damascus to the synagogues, that if he found any of this way, whether they were men or women, he might bring them bound unto Jerusalem."[71]

Doubt.

[71] Acts 9:2

Damascus is about one hundred and fifty miles north of Jerusalem, so it would take Saul and his attendants about a week to travel the distance. Perhaps during those few days of comparative leisure, he began to wonder whether what he was doing was right or not. Perhaps the shining face of the dying Stephen and the martyr's last prayer began to sink more deeply into his soul than it had done before. Little children's cries for their parents whom Saul had bound began to pierce his soul more keenly, and make him feel miserably unhappy as he looked forward to more experiences of that kind in Damascus. Perhaps he wondered whether the work of the Lord, if he were really engaged in it, would make him feel so restless and bitter. He was soon to learn that only the work of the evil one produces those feelings, and that true service for the Lord, always brings peace and contentment.

Light.

But, whatever his thoughts and feelings were, he was hastening on with a determination to arrest every follower of Jesus whom he could find. As he neared the city, however, "suddenly there shined round about him a light from heaven." Saul fell to the earth, and the men with him stood around him speechless.

From that moment, Saul was a changed man. When he fell to the earth, he was a proud, haughty Pharisee, a persecutor of innocent people: when he arose, he was a humble, submissive seeker after truth, a repentant follower of Him whom he had been persecuting. From the midst of the light, came a voice saying:

The Revelation.

"Saul, Saul, why persecutest thou me?"

"Who art thou, Lord?" asked Saul.

"I am Jesus whom thou persecutest," and then He added, in effect. "The more you persecute me the worse you feel; and the more your conscience troubles you." Fighting the Lord is just like kicking a "prickly pear," the harder you kick the worse it hurts.

When Saul realized this, and knew he had been doing wrong, he asked, "What wilt Thou have me to do?"

A Commission.

"Arise, go into the city, and it will be told thee what thou must do," not what Saul would like to do; not what he might do; but what he *must* do, if he would be accepted of the Lord.

Eyes but Saw Not; Blind, but Sees.

Saul had been blessed with eyesight but had been blinded spiritually. Now he was blind physically, but light was coming into his soul. As he arose he could see nothing, and his attendants led him into the city, where he lodged in the house of Judas, in a street called Straight.

Ananias.

In the meantime, the Lord, in a vision, said to one of His servants called Ananias, "Arise and go into the street called Straight, and inquire in the house of Judas for one called Saul, of Tarsus: for, behold, he prayeth."

But Ananias answered, "Lord, I have heard by many of this man, how much evil he hath done to Thy saints of Jerusalem: and here he hath authority from the chief priests to bind all that call on Thy name." Ananias was probably one whom Saul would have arrested first.

The Lord told Ananias to go as directed, for He had chosen Saul to bear His name, "before the Gentiles, and kings, and the children of Israel."

Saul Administered to.

Ananias did as directed; and when he entered the house of Judas, he found Saul not only penitent but blind. All the proud Pharisee's bitterness was gone and he was praying for light—light in his eyes and light in his soul. His prayers were answered, for God's humble servant laid his hands upon him and said, "Brother Saul, the Lord, even Jesus that appeared unto thee in the way as thou camest, hath sent me, that thou mightest receive thy sight, and be filled with the Holy Ghost."

Receives Sight.

And Saul received his sight immediately, and arose and was baptized. This was one thing he had to do if he would be numbered in the Church of Christ. Thus in the conversion of this great man, we find illustrated the application of several principles of the Gospel, viz.: Faith, in Jesus Christ; Repentance from wrong doing; Baptism and the recognition of Christ's authority on earth.

LESSON 24 IN ANOTHER SCHOOL

"All the scholastic scaffolding falls as a ruined edifice, before one single word—faith."

Teachers Compared.

For several days immediately following his wonderful conversion and his restoration to sight, Saul "was with the disciples who were at Damascus." Saul had now entered another school, but how different from the one in which he sat at the feet of the learned Gamaliel! There he listened to instruction from the most learned men of his day; now he is listening to men who were thought unlearned. There he received training of the intellect; now he is receiving training of the soul. There he studied blindly; now he studies, truly seeing! His instructor is one of the faithful men whom he had despised and whom he came to arrest. "Not Peter, or James or John, no great and eminent apostle need be sent for, to instruct the learned and highly talented Saul; but Ananias, some poor, simple-hearted Christian of whom the Divine word has never before made mention, is fully sufficient, in God's hand, to teach this most richly endowed of all the early converts."

True Zeal.

As he listened, hour after hour, during those few memorable days, his soul became fired with a true zeal; and we can imagine hearing him say to his new teachers,

"Set on your foot. And with a heart new fir'd I follow you."

"And straightway he preached Christ in the synagogues, that He is the Son of God."

Jews Amazed.

We are not told whether any of the men who accompanied him to Damascus became converted. Perhaps one or two did; but, undoubtedly, some of them thought Saul had turned traitor. So also did the Jews in Damascus, who were amazed, and said to one another, "Is not this he that destroyed them which called on this name in Jerusalem, and came here for that intent, that he might bring them bound unto the chief priests?" But the more they opposed him, the more eloquently he defended the name of Jesus and proved to them that Jesus is the Christ.

The School of Solitude.

After a few days of fiery disputations in the synagogues, Saul concluded to leave Damascus and go into retirement; so, bidding his new friends goodby, he went into Arabia in the mountains near the Red Sea. Here he received instruction in the School of Solitude.

"O sacred solitude! divine retreat!
Choice of the prudent! envy of the great!
By thy Pure stream, or in thy waving shade,
We court fair wisdom."

Like Moses, Elijah, John the Baptist, and even the Savior Himself, Paul now sought to be alone with God, and to learn how to get his spirit in communion with the Holy Spirit.

How long he remained there, we do not know. All he says about this journey is: "I went into Arabia, and returned again to Damascus."

HIS FLIGHT FROM DAMASCUS

No sooner had he returned to the city of his conversion, than he began to preach again in the synagogues. Again the Jews began to dispute him, and again he confounded them. Day after day, and week after week the religious controversy continued until the Jews could stand it no longer, and "took council to kill him."

Every Gate Guarded.

Around the city of Damascus was a high wall, and no one could go in or out except through the gates. Therefore, when the Jews decided to kill Saul, the first thing they did was to make sure he could not escape. So they placed guards at every gate, and "watched day and night to kill him."

Friends.

But Saul had his friends as well as enemies, and he had one Friend who had chosen him for a great and useful mission, and as long as Saul was faithful, his life would be spared until this special work was done. Through inspiration or otherwise, Saul knew that his enemies were lying in wait for him, so he kept out of their way.

Over the Wall.

Fortunately, one of his friends lived in a house built right near the wall of the city; and from here, some of the disciples assisted Saul to escape. They put him in a basket, and then watching carefully to see that no enemies were in sight, they carried Saul to the top of the wall, and let him down on the other side. Thus it happened that while the wicked guards were watching day and night to entrap Saul, that disciple of the Master was making his journey back to Jerusalem.

WITH THE DISCIPLES IN JERUSALEM

Returns to Jerusalem.

Three years before, he left Jerusalem as an officer of the Sanhedrin, bearing a special commission, and accompanied by attendants and officers. He left with enmity in his heart for every person who professed to believe in Jesus Christ. Now he journeys back alone, rejected by those whom he had served, a fugitive from the Jews who, a few years before, awaited to welcome him as a hero! But Saul is happier now alone as he is than when he went in pomp to arrest God's servants. And yet he can look forward to no welcome in Jerusalem! His old friends and teachers think he has turned traitor to their cause, and the Apostles of Jesus doubt his conversion. "They were all afraid of him, and believed not that he was a disciple."

Barnabas.

But there was one, an old friend and true, a classmate, and fellow townsman who extended to Saul the glad hand of fellowship. That was Barnabas, who "took him, and brought him to the apostles," declaring how Saul had been converted by a light, and the voice of the Lord, and how he had preached in Damascus in the name of Jesus.

With this testimony, the Apostles accepted Saul, and gave him their companionship. Soon Saul was preaching in Jerusalem as boldly as he had in Damascus. In his disputes with the Grecians, he evidently confounded them as he had those in Damascus, and with the same effect—"They went about to slay him."

Back to Tarsus.

When the brethren learned this, "they brought him down to Caesarea, and sent him forth to Tarsus" back to his old home, to his parents and to his sister. But what a changed man from what he was when he left to practice in Jerusalem. In name he was still "Saul of Tarsus;" but in nature he was Paul the disciple of Jesus Christ.

CALLED TO ASSIST BARNABAS

During the persecution in which Stephen was martyred, the Saints scattered to different places, and where ever they went, they preached the Glad Tidings of Great Joy. "And the hand of the Lord was with them, and a great number believed and turned unto the Lord."

Christians.

A large number of these converts gathered in Antioch and it was there as you already know that the Saints were first called Christians. It was first applied to them in derision just as the word "Mormon" was first applied to the Church in this day, but later was accepted as an honorable title.

Barnabas Seeks Saul.

Barnabas, who "was a good man, and full of the Holy Ghost and of faith" was appointed to look after the Saints in that great city. Finding a great missionary opportunity in that field, and desiring able assistance in carrying on the great work assigned him, Barnabas decided to go to Tarsus, his old home, and try to find Paul. What a happy time these old playmates must have had when they met once again in the familiar scenes of their boyhood days! We are not told what they did, nor what they said, nor what their old friends and relatives thought of their new religion. We do know, however, that Paul accepted the call to go with Barnabas to Antioch. There "they assembled themselves in the Church, and taught much people." This seems to have been Paul's first definite assignment in the Church.

LESSON 25 SPECIAL MESSENGERS TO JERUSALEM

"God has so ordered that men, being in need of each other, should learn to love each other, and bear each other's burdens."
"To pity distress is but human; to relieve it is God-like."

Agabus.

While Paul and Barnabas were at Antioch, there came "prophets from Jerusalem," one of whom was named Agabus. He is thought to have been one of the Seventy chosen by the Savior; but just what priesthood and what position in the Church he held we do not know for certain. But he must have been a righteous man, and filled with the Holy Ghost, for he could foretell, through the inspiration of the Spirit, things that other people, by their own intelligence, could not see. At the time of which we are speaking he prophesied that "there should be a great dearth throughout all the world," meaning that there would be a famine in the land, and that people would go hungry.

Offerings to Poor.

The disciples had faith in Agabus and believed to be true what he said. They knew of some of the Saints in Judea who could not stand a famine; in fact, many of them had given all they had to the Church; so "every man according to his ability determined to send relief unto the brethren who dwelt in Judea." Paul and Barnabas were chosen as the messengers of relief.

Famine.

It was well they did so, for the famine came just as Agabus had said it would. Luke tells us that it happened in the days of Claudius Caesar (44 A. D.), and profane historians inform us that it was so severe that even the emperor himself was insulted in the market place by those who were starving.

Persecution Under Herod.

At about the time that the two elders were sent from Antioch to Jerusalem, there was a bitter persecution, waged against the Saints; and "Herod the king began to vex certain of the Church, and he killed James, the brother of John, with the sword." Those were the days in which Peter was imprisoned and chained to his guards, but through the miraculous intervention of God, was delivered by an angel. Paul and Barnabas were probably present in the house of Mary the mother of John Mark, joining in prayer for the preservation of Peter's life, when, as we have already learned in the lessons on Peter, Rhoda announced Peter at the door.

Return to Caesarea.

After witnessing this wonderful manifestation of the power of God in behalf of His servants, Paul and Barnabas probably witnessed how God sometimes punishes the wicked. If so, it happened on this wise. Their duty as messengers for the Saints in Antioch had been faithfully performed, and the relief sent to the members of the Church in Judea properly delivered to those who should have it in charge. They had spent many days renewing old friendships, and enjoying the companionship, even in persecution, of the leaders and members of the Church of Christ. They were now ready to return and report their labors to the Church in Antioch. Their return journey took them to Caesarea. Perhaps they visited Cornelius, whose home, you remember, was there. At any rate, some who have carefully studied the life and travels of St. Paul tell us that on his return from Jerusalem at this time, he witnessed the death of the wicked King Herod. Weed describes the scene as follows:

Death of Herod.

"The Roman Emperor Claudius had obtained great victories in Great Britain. On his return to Rome there was great rejoicing. Herod thought he would gain great favor with the emperor by a grand festival in his honor in Caesarea, to which he hastened from Jerusalem. On the morning of the second day the theatre was filled with a mass of human beings to witness the inhuman exhibition of gladiators who fought one another for public amusement. Herod appeared in a magnificent robe, sparkling with silver. As the rays of the early morning sun fell upon him, the eyes of the beholders were dazzled by the brilliant robe. Flattered by their foolish cries of admiration he made an oration to the people who gave a shout, crying, 'It is the voice of a God and not of a man.' He was willing to be so called, though this was blasphemy, giving to a man what belongs to God alone. "Immediately the angel of the Lord smote him because he gave not God the glory." This was very different from the experience of Peter in prison when the angel of the Lord came upon him, and smote him upon the side; and led him from death.

"The smiting of Herod by the angel was with a dreadful disease such as had caused the death of his grandfather. He was carried from the theatre to his palace where he lingered five days in agony until death closed his life in the fifty-fourth year of his age. It was the fourth year of his reign over the region where had ruled his grandfather, whose wicked example he had followed to a like inglorious end."

"When in the theatre the scene was suddenly changed from the gladiatorial and other wicked amuesements to the judgment on the king, the multitude fled, rending their clothes according to the custom in horror."

John Mark.

All these things and many more, Paul and Barnabas would report to the Saints upon their return to Antioch. Luke informs us that after they had fulfilled their ministry they returned from Jerusalem, and "took with them John whose surname was Mark."

The Report.

Interesting meetings were held in Antioch, at which the report of the mission of Paul and Barnabas was given. In attendance at these meetings and reasiding in Antioch at the time were certain prophets and teachers, Barnabas, and Lucius of Cyrene, and Manean, which had been brought up with Herod the tetrarch, and Saul. As they ministered to the Lord, and fasted, the Holy Ghost said, "separate me Barnabas and Saul for the work whereunto I have called them." They had performed one duty well and faithfully, and were now better prepared for a greater one for which the Lord had chosen them. This was a special mission to the Gentiles.

Some time later, after fasting and prayer, some of the prophets and teachers laid their hands on the chosen missionaries, set them apart, and bade them prepare for their journey.

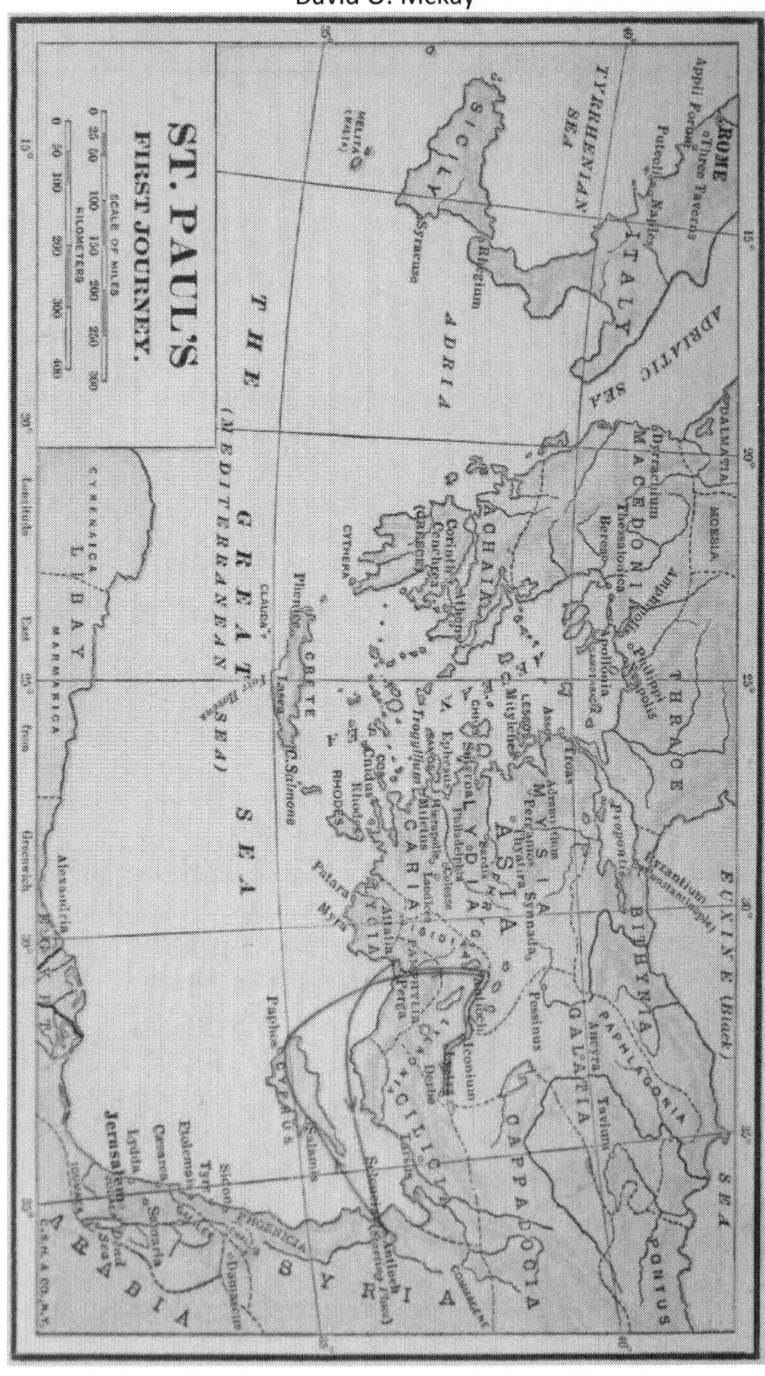
ST. PAUL'S
FIRST JOURNEY.
SCALE OF MILES
KILOMETERS
Longitude East from Greenwich
ROME
Appii Forum
Three Taverns
Puteoli
Naples
TYRRHENIAN SEA
SICILY
Syracuse
Rhegium
ITALY
ADRIATIC SEA
ADRIA
THE GREAT SEA
(MEDITERRANEAN SEA)
DALMATIA
MOESIA
MACEDONIA
Dyrrachium
Thessalonica
Berea
ACHAIA
Corinth
Athens
CYTHERA
THRACE
Amphipolis
Philippi
Neapolis
Apollonia
Troas
Assos
Mitylene
LESBOS
MYSIA
ASIA
Thyatira
LYDIA
Ephesus
Philadelphia
Miletus
Laodicea
Colosse
CARIA
Cnidus
RHODES
Patara
Myra
LYCIA
Attalia
Perga
Iconium
Lystra
Derbe
CILICIA
Tarsus
Paphos
CYPRUS
Salamis
Seleucia
Antioch
SYRIA
Damascus
PHOENICIA
Sidon
Tyre
Ptolemais
Caesarea
Samaria
Lydda
Jerusalem
ARABIA
EUXINE (Black) SEA
Byzantium (Constantinople)
Propontis
BITHYNIA
PAPHLAGONIA
GALATIA
Pessinus
Ancyra
Tavium
PONTUS
CAPPADOCIA
CRETE
Lasea
C. Salmone
CLAUDA
CYRENAICA
LYBIA
MARMARICA
Alexandria

LESSON 26 FIRST MISSIONARY JOURNEY

"Let your religion be seen. Lamps do not talk, but they do shine. A lighthouse sounds no drum, it beats no gong; yet far over the waters its friendly light is seen by the mariner."

Soon after the special meetings mentioned in the last chapter, Paul, Barnabas and John Mark started on their mission, which is now known as Paul's first missionary tour.

At Cyprus.

Leaving the famous city of Antioch, in Syria, they sailed down the river to Seleucia, a seaport town on the Mediterranean Sea. Here they took the boat on the open sea, and sailed southwestward to the island of Cyprus.

At Salamis.

Landing at Salamis, a port of Cyprus, the missionaries began their labors at once, preaching the word of God in the synagogue of the Jews. Here Barnabas was at home, and undoubtedly experienced great joy in preaching the Gospel to his old friends and playmates. But he must have been deeply grieved to see how many of them rejected his message, and continued in sin and idolatry.

The Gentiles on this island worshiped the goddess Venus, to whom they built a temple and offered sacrifices.

Call to Repentance.

Their religion, instead of making them purer in their thoughts and more virtuous in their actions, made them more sinful. So Paul and his companions found the people very wicked indeed. Wherever they went, these three missionaries preached the only true Gospel, and called on men "everywhere to repent."

They traveled the entire length of Cyprus, a distance of one hundred miles, telling the people about Christ the Redeemer of the world.

AT PAPHOS

Governor Hears Gospel.

On the southwestern coast of Cyprus was the chief city of the island named Paphos. Here is where the Roman governor, or, as Luke says, the "deputy of the country," lived. As was their custom, soon after the missionaries entered the city they proclaimed their message to the people. When the governor, Sergius Paulus, heard about them, he "called for Barnabas and Paul, and desired to hear the word of God." Luke says he was "a prudent man," so we conclude that he was sincere in his desire to know the truth.

ELYMAS THE SORCERER

A Sorcerer Rejects Gospel.

But there was living in the deptuy-house at the time a man who was not sincere, and who claimed to be a sorcerer. He rejected Paul's message, and opposed his teachings. Bar-Jesus was his right name, and he was a Jew, and a false prophet. Paul read his wicked heart, and knew that because of selfishness and love of money he rejected the Gospel.

"Then Paul, filled with the Holy Ghost, set his eyes on him and said, O full of subtlety and all mischief, thou child of the devil, thou enemy of all righteousness, wilt thou not cease to pervert the right ways of the Lord?

"And now behold the hand of the Lord is upon thee, and thou shalt be blind, not seeing the sun for a season.

"And immediately there fell on him a mist and a darkness; and he went about seeking some one to lead him by the hand."

If in his darkness he had let the messengers of Light lead him they would have given him eternal sight, just as Paul had received it through Ananias, in Damascus. But we are led to believe that he remained blind and bitter.

The Governor Believes.

Sergius Paulus, however, believed, "being astonished at the doctrine of the Lord." Many others believed also, and in the wicked town of Paphos, where the revellers worshiped the goddess of love, a church was organized, and a little body of Christians came together to worship the true God and His Son Jesus Christ.

IN PAMPHYLIA

A Missionary Returns.

From Paphos, Paul and his companions sailed northward to Perga in Pamphylia. At this place something happened about which we wish we knew more. All that Luke says about it is this:

"And John departing from there returned to Jerusalem."

We know that later, this circumstance became a matter of sharp dispute between Barnabas and Paul, but just why John wished to return we are not informed. Perhaps he had not intended to travel so far; or it may be that matters at home needed his attention; or he might have been over sensitive, and felt that "two were company but three were a crowd;" but whatever the cause Paul and Barnabas had to continue their journey without the young man Mark. Later, he resumed his missionary work traveling with Barnabas. There is no record of his traveling again with Paul; although the latter wrote of him later as "a comfort, and a fellow worker unto the kingdom of God."

IN PISIDIA

Through Mountain Passes.

From Perga in Pamphylia, Paul and Barnabas continued north to Antioch in Pisidia. Day after day, these two missionaries traveled on foot through a mountainous region, where very few people resided. Sometimes, perhaps, they could find lodging with some shepherd, but more often, they would sleep in caves or among the trees. But they had a message of salvation in their hearts and so were happy. After about seven days of wearisome and dangerous travel, they reached Antioch in Pisidia.

In the Synagogue.

When the Sabbath day came, as was their custom, the missionaries went into the synagogue, and sat down in the congregation. After the leaders had read the law and the prophets, they asked the visitors if they had "any word of exhortation for the people." At this, Paul stood up and delivered a most impressive sermon, so much so, that the people invited Paul to speak again on the next Sabbath. Many who were present accepted the Gospel.[72]

"And the next Sabbath day came almost the whole city together to hear the word of God.

Turn to Gentiles.

"But when the Jews saw the multitudes, they were filled with envy, and spake against those things which were spoken by Paul, contradicting and blaspheming." Their opposition and contradiction made the missionaries only more earnest and emphatic. Finally, when it was apparent that the Jews would not accept the truth, Paul and Barnabas waxed bold and said, "It was necessary that the word of God should first have been spoken to you; but seeing ye put it from you, and judge yourselves unworthy of everlasting life, lo we turn to the Gentiles." When the Gentiles heard this announcement, they were delighted and many of them accepted the principles of the Gospel.

Jews Jealous.

But the Jews were jealous; they became filled with envy and determined to drive the missionaries "out of their coasts." This they

---

[72] See Paul's sermon, Acts 13:14-41.

did with the aid of "the devout and honorable women and the chief men of the city." The persecution became so bitter that Paul and Barnabas "shook off the dust of their feet against them, and came unto Iconium."

IN ICONIUM

Again in Synagogue.

Filled with the joy that comes from true service to one's fellowmen, Paul and Barnabas began their preaching in Iconium. Entering the synagogue here, as they had done in the city from which they had just been driven, they spoke "boldly in the Lord, who gave testimony unto the word of His grace, and granted signs and wonders to be done by their hands."

Again Opposed.

Jews and Greeks also rallied around the standard as unfurled by these great missionaries; but Jews and Greeks also organized to oppose them. The result was that the city was divided; "and part held with the Jews and part with the Apostles."

Hearing that a plot was on foot to do them injury, and to stone them, Paul and Barnabas withdrew from the city, and went to "Lystra and Derbe, cities of Lycaonia, and unto the region that lieth round about."

LESSON 27 FIRST MISSIONARY JOURNEY—Continued

AT LYSTRA AND DERBE

"Outward attacks and troubles rather fix than unsettle the Christian, as tempests from without only serve to root the oak more firmly in the ground."

"As sure as ever God puts His children in the furnace, He will be in the furnace with them."

Among the Heathen.

At Lystra, Paul and Barnabas found a people who were almost entirely heathen for they worshiped Jupiter and Mercury and other false deities, and knew little or nothing about the true God. There were Jews amongst them, but not of sufficient numbers even to build a synagogue.

The country was wild and rugged, and the inhabitants were like the country. They were "villagers of little learning, and rude in dress and manner." Such people are usually shy of strangers, and slow to accept anything new. But once they begin to get confidence in the stranger, they may be easily swayed by him; not having very definite opinions of their own.

The doctrine preached by Paul and Barnabas was new to them, and after a time began to arouse their curiosity, and then awaken their interest.

Choice People Among Them.

Some of the most intelligent comprehended the truth, and accepted it. Lest you boys and girls might think that there were no superior people among these heathens, you must be reminded of the fact that in Lystra there was at least one choice family of whose membership in the Church the Bible makes mention, and in Derbe there were others.

Timothy.

In these towns, out of the persecution and affliction heaped upon them by the ignorant and wicked, Paul and Barnabas brought to the faith some of the choicest members of the early Church. Among these were Timothy, whom Paul afterwards called his son; Eunice, Timothy's mother, and Lois, Timothy's grandmother, whose "unfeigned faith" Paul commended in later years. Undoubtedly, the friendship alone of these noble people more than paid Paul for all the persecution he suffered during this first mission.

But to the people generally, the message was strange and incomprehensisble. They could not separate the doctrine of Christ from their heathen deities as was shown by a remarkable experience.

A Miracle.

Paul and Barnabas and a few converts were holding a meeting one day in the "open air." In the audience sat a man "impotent in his feet," who had been a cripple from birth, and who had never walked. This fact, of course, all the people knew, for many of them were acquainted with him, and had seen him carried to the meeting. "The same heard Paul speak," and conviction entered his weary heart that what Paul said was true. Paul looked at him, and "perceiving that he had faith to be healed," said, "Stand upright on thy feet." This he commanded by the power of the Redeemer.

Effect.

"The man leaped to his feet and walked." When the people saw this, they created an uproar in the city, and they said in their language, which was a mixture of Greek and Syrian:

"The gods have come down to us in the likeness of men," and they named Paul and Barnabas after their gods. Barnabas was tall, so they called him Jupiter; and Paul, being short and a gifted speaker, they called Mercury, because Mercury was supposed to preside over learning and eloquence.

To Offer Sacrifice

Some time after the meeting, the priests of Jupiter, who officiated in the temple of Jupiter that was in the city, decided to offer sacrifice to their gods as personified in Paul and Barnabas. So with the people, they gathered at the gates of the city, brought oxen and began to prepare to offer sacrifice.

Missionaries Protest.

When Paul and Barnabas heard of it, they ran among the people, and "rent their clothes" in protestation against such sacrifice. To rend their clothes was to express intense feeling and the people so understood it. Besides doing this they cried: "Sirs, why do ye these things? We also are men of like passions with you, and preach unto you that ye should turn from these vanities unto the living God, which made heaven and earth, and the sea, and all things that are therein."

Paul Stoned.

However, they could scarcely make the people refrain from worshiping them; but there were certain Jews there who had followed the missionaries from Antioch and Iconium, "who persuaded the people" that Paul and Barnabas were deceivers, and that the miracle which had been performed had been done by the power of the evil one. These Jews swayed the people to such an extent that instead of worshiping Paul and Barnabas, they picked up stones and stoned Paul until he fell to the earth, apparently dead. Thinking he was so, the mob then dragged his body out of the city and left it.

A Many Headed Monster.

What a many-headed monster this mob was! First they were ready to worship the men as gods, and then in just a few minutes became so bitter that they would stain their souls with murder! Shakespeare called such a crowd

> "The blind monster, with uncounted heads.
> The still discordant, wavering multitude."

Paul Regains Consciousness.

The mob dispersed, and around the still bleeding, silent body on the ground, stood the few intelligent, faithful disciples who had believed the true Gospel. How delighted and thankful they must have been when they saw Paul move, and later regain consciousness.

He had been stunned, but not seriously injured; so a little gentle nursing gave him strength to stand on his feet, and he walked back to the city.

Gaius.

The next day he left Lystra and traveled twenty miles to Derbe. Here he preached boldly and effectively, and converted many to the truth, among them a man by the name of Gaius, who proved to be a staunch and true friend to Paul and to the Church generally.

Another Branch Organized.

As they had done in other cities, so the missionaries did in Derbe—organized a branch of the Church and ordained elders over it. These they instructed, and met with them and with the Saints in fasting and prayer, "commended them to the Lord," and bade them goodby, for the time had come when the first missionaries from Antioch should return home.

Return Home.

They visited all the branches, preaching the Gospel, instructing, blessing, and comforting the Saints in Lystra and the regions round about. They then returned forty miles to Iconium and sixty miles back to Antioch in Pisidia. From there, they went to Perga in Pamphylia, and sailed from Attalia to Antioch in Syria.

Here the Saints gathered and bade them welcome, and heard the returned Elders report "all that God had done with them, and how He had opened the door of faith unto the Gentiles."

LESSON 28 A GREAT CONTROVERSY

Texts: Acts 15:1-35

"The union of Christians to Christ, their common head, and by means of the influence they derive from Him, one to another, may be illustrated by the loadstone. It not only attaches the particles of iron to itself by the magnetic virtue, but by this virtue it unites them one to the other."

Jews Scattered Over Empire.

As we followed Paul and Barnabas in their first missionary journey, we noticed that in nearly every city they visited, they found Jews, and that their preaching was frequently first done in a synagogue. The fact is, that the Jews were scattered over nearly all of the Roman Empire. They were on the coasts and islands of Western Asia, on the borders of the Caspian Sea, and some were even as far as China.

Jews Kept to Their Religion.

But no matter where the Jew was living, he always kept his own religion, and studied carefully the Law of Moses. That is what James meant when he said, "Moses of old time, hath in every city, them that preach him, being read in the synagogues every Sabbath day." Their religion taught them not to mingle with the Gentiles in marriage or in social intercourse.

Gentiles Would Not Worship With Jews.

The Gentiles, on the other hand, looked with contempt upon the Jews; while the "gay and licentious festivities of the Greek and Roman worship" made the Jews look with contempt upon Gentiles. They would trade with each other, and mingle together in daily vocations, but as a rule, that is as far as their intercourse went. They said with Shylock: "I will buy with you, sell with you, talk with you, walk with you, and so following; but I will not eat with you, drink with you, nor pray with you."[73]

Of course, there were Gentiles who sometimes became converted to the Jewish religion, and there were some who married Jewish women, but the line of dislike and suspicion was none the less sharply drawn.

[73] Merchant of Venice; Act 1, Scene 3.

Peter's Prejudices.

You remember how difficult it was for the Lord to convince Peter that the Gentiles were worthy to be baptized into the Church of Christ. Peter saw in a vision a vast sheet descending from heaven in which there were unclean animals, and he heard a voice saying, "Arise, Peter, kill and eat." But Peter said, "Not so, Lord: for I have never eaten anything that is common or unclean."[74]

Peter's Revelation.

When Peter realized the meaning of the vision, his whole Jewish nature was shocked; for to obey was to break the Law of his forefathers by associating with Gentiles. The Jewish Christians who were with Peter from Joppa to Caesarea were "astonished" when they saw "the gift of the Holy Ghost poured out" on the "unclean" Gentiles. When Peter reached Jerusalem, he was accused of having not only associated but eaten with Gentiles, but Peter had learned by revelation that "what God has made clean" no one should "call common or unclean," that the Lord is "no respecter of persons," and that "every nation" that accepts Him, and "feareth Him and worketh righteousness," may receive His blessings.

THE QUESTION AGITATED

The Church Agitated.

But there were many Jews in the Church who did not believe this, and the only condition on which they would accept a Gentile was that he should obey the Jewish religion also. When this class of Christians heard that Paul and Barnabas had baptized hundreds of Gentiles, they became very much agitated in their feelings, and some of them went to Antioch and began to preach, first privately then publicly, that unless the Gentiles obeyed a certain Jewish rite, they could not be saved. Paul and Barnabas had told the Saints that obedience to the Gospel of Christ would save the Gentiles as well as the Jews, and that the Gentiles did not have to become Jews. Now these men from the chief branch of the Church declared that Paul and Barnabas were wrong. No wonder "those who from among the Gentiles were turned unto God," were "troubled" and perplexed. Indeed, the controversy became so sharp that it threatened to lead some out of the Church.

MESSENGERS SENT TO JERUSALEM

Messengers to Jerusalem.

---

[74] Review entire experience.

So it was "determined that Paul and Barnabas, and certain other of them, should go up to Jerusalem unto the apostles and elders about this question."

The Church in Antioch evidently believed Paul and Barnabas to be in the right, for when they started on their journey they were escorted on their way by the Church. As they passed through Syro-Phoenecia and Samaria, and told the Saints who greeted them how the Gentiles had been converted, they "caused great joy unto all the brethren."

Paul's Third Visit.

This was Paul's third visit to Jerusalem since his conversion. The first was three years after he joined the Church, when he spent two weeks with Peter, and then had to flee for his life. The second was when he accompanied the messengers who brought relief to the Saints in Judea during the famine. That was the time Peter was sentenced to be killed. Fifteen years had passed since he left Jerusalem for Damascus with papers to arrest all Christians whom he found! Now he enters the city as the defender of one of the greatest truths that the Christian Church or the world can know; namely, that God is no respecter of persons, but will bless every nation as it obeys the principles of life and salvation.

IN COUNCIL WITH THE LEADERS

Titus.

He first met in council with Peter, James and John, and received for the first time, so far as we know, "the right hand of fellowship" from John the beloved disciple. Titus was with Paul as an example of those who were Gentile converts.

An Appeal to the Presidency.

This visit was really an appeal to the Presidency of the Twelve, and confirms the belief of the members of the Church today that Peter, James and John were appointed leaders at that time just as three High Priests are now chosen as the First Presidency of Christ's Church.

An Important Meeting.

At length the great meeting was called at which was to be settled once and for all the standing of the Gentiles in the Christian Church. "It was a scene of earnest debate, and perhaps, in its earlier portion, of angry disputing"; but finally Peter addressed the assembly, and told how God had revealed to him the fact that the Gentiles could accept the Gospel without obeying all the Jewish ceremonies.

Missionaries Testify.

Then Paul and Barnabas spoke amidst great silence, while every eye was riveted upon these two great missionaries who had first organized branches of the Church among Gentile nations.

The Decision.

Finally, James, the brother of the Lord, who was known among the Jews as "James the Just," arose and gave the decision of the council, which established the union of the Jewish and the Gentile Christians.

PAUL RETURNS TO ANTIOCH

Judas and Silas.

Thus the controversy ended, and Paul's mission to the Gentiles was authoritatively approved. When he started back to Antioch he was accompanied by Judas surnamed Barsabas and Silas, "chief men among the brethren." It seems that John Mark went with them also. They carried with them the decree of the council to be read to the churches that had been so disturbed by the controversy.

When they reached Antioch, the whole body of the church met together, to hear the decision of the council. We can imagine with what interest and consolation the saints listened to the decree that there should not be one Church for the Jew and another for the Gentile; but that everyone who sincerely believed in Christ, and obeyed the Gospel would be saved.

LESSON 29 PAUL BEGINS HIS SECOND MISSIONARY JOURNEY

"Man should trust in God, as if God did all, and yet labor as earnestly as if he himself did all."

Paul Desires to Visit Branches.

After Silas and Judas Barsabas had remained in Antioch a short time "teaching and preaching the word of the Lord" with Paul and Barnabas and "many others also," Judas returned presumably to Jerusalem, but it "pleased Silas to abide there still." Two years had passed since Paul and Barnabas had returned from their first mission, and Paul felt impressed to visit again the churches they had established on that memorable tour. So one day he said to Barnabas. "Let us go again and visit our brethren in every city where we have preached the word of the Lord, and see how they do."

Disagreement.

To this Barnabas readily consented, but said, "Let us take my cousin John Mark along with us." "No," answered Paul, "it is not good to take Mark with us, because he turned back from us at Pamphylia, and went not with us to the work."

Separation.

But Barnabas knew why Mark had done that, and was sure he would not turn back this time. Paul, however, would not consent; so these two great missionaries agreed to separate, and each take his own companion. Barnabas chose John Mark, and Paul chose Silas. They probably also agreed that Barnabas and Mark should go to the churches on the islands, and Paul and Silas to those on the mainland.

We do not know that Paul and Barnabas ever met again, but Paul speaks of him afterwards as of an apostle actively engaged in his Master's service. Mark, too, in later years won Paul's confidence, for the latter speaks of him as his "fellow-laborer," and one "profitable to the ministry."

Barnabas and Mark at Cyprus.

Barnabas and Mark left first, and sailed to Cyprus, Barnabas' native island. Here Mark, too, would feel at home, for it was where he began his work as a missionary. Here we will leave them among the newly-made Christians, and follow Paul and Silas.

PROBABLE VISIT TO PAUL'S OLD HOME

These two missionaries started by land northward through "Syria and Cilicia, confirming the churches." They had with them, of course, the decision of the Council which no doubt, gave a great deal of comfort to the Christian Gentiles in these branches.

Paul and Silas.

Just what particular cities Paul and Silas visited in Syria and Cilicia, we do not know; but there was one which Paul certainly would not pass by. Paul and That was his old home town Tarsus. If he had succeeded in establishing a church there, with what joy and satisfaction he would return to it now. Paul was always proud of Tarsus, and spoke of it later as "no mean city."[75]

TIMOTHY.

"Instructed from childhood to read the scripture, and to lead a pure life."

[75] Acts 21:39.

AT DERBE AND OTHER TOWNS

Derbe First.

On his first mission, Paul and Barnabas visited in order Iconium, Lystra, and Derbe, Now he and Silas approach these towns from the opposite direction, and come to Derbe first, then to Lystra, then to Iconium.

Welcome at Lystra.

At Lystra he was welcomed by that beautiful character Eunice who was a Jewess, the mother of Timothy. Lois, her mother, would also greet Paul, and extend the glad hand to his companion Silas.

CALL AND ORDINATION OF TIMOTHY

Timothy True to Faith.

From the brethren at Iconium and Lystra, Paul learned that these good women and their noble young son Timothy had been true to the faith. He already knew that Timothy had been instructed from childhood to repeat the scripture and to live a pure life. Timothy had been one who had stood by him when the mob dragged him from the city and left him for dead, and now he finds still in the young man's heart the "unfeigned faith which first dwelt in his grandmother Lois, and his mother Eunice." No wonder Paul said to the women "I desire Timothy to go forth with me."

Timothy Ordained.

The mother consented, and Timothy accepted the call, though scarcely twenty years of age. Accordingly, a meeting was held, and Paul ordained Timothy by "the laying on of hands" to be a missionary and servant of the Lord Jesus Christ. Paul afterwards called this young man his "own son in the Faith."[76] This instance tends to confirm the truth of the Article of Faith which declares the belief of the Latter-day Saints that "a man must be called of God, by prophecy and by the laying on of hands, by those who are in authority, to preach the Gospel and administer in the ordinances thereof."

Towards Galatia.

After baptizing many more converts and establishing the churches in the faith, and undoubtedly visiting Antioch in Pisidia and other towns on the mainland where he and Barnabas had organized branches of the Church, Paul, Silas, and Timothy went in a northerly direction through "the region of Galatia."

---

[76] I Tim. 1:2.

Paul Ill.

While passing through here Paul was taken sick. What kind of sickness, whether it was "the thorn in the flesh" he mentions in one of his epistles, or some other bodily ailment, is not stated. Paul calls it an "infirmity of the flesh."[77] But he was very sick, and was detained in Galatia seemingly against his will. In spite of sickness, however, he preached the Gospel to the people and many believed. How he loved the friends he made at that time, and appreciated their tender care, can be partly understood from a letter he wrote to them in which he said in effect, "When I was sick in your midst, ye despised me not, nor rejected; but received me as an angel of God, even as Christ Jesus. What was then the blessedness ye spake of? for I bear you record, that, if it had been possible, ye would have plucked out your own eyes, and have given them to me."[78] In that same letter he calls them his "little children,"[79] and expresses a desire to be with them again to strengthen them in the Gospel.

Branches Established.

Before the missionaries left Galatia, even though Paul suffered in sickness, several new branches of the Church had been organized, and Paul's letter to these churches now forms part of the New Testament.

Westward.

Leaving Galatia, the three travelers continued westward toward the Aegean Sea, and "passing by Mysia came to Troas," the full name of which was Alexandria Troas.

Paul had his face turned toward Europe and from this place could look across the Aegean and see the "distant prospect of the Macedonian hills."

A Vision.

One evening he went to bed, perhaps wondering about the people who lived on the other side of the water and inspired with the feeling that the Lord desired him to go to them. There appeared to him, that night, a vision, in which "There stood a man of Macedonia, and prayed him, saying,

"Come over into Macedonia, and help us."

---

[77] Gal. 4:13.
[78] Gal. 4:13-15.
[79] Gal. 2:19.

Luke.

But before he took boat across, he and his companions had been joined by another faithful convert to whom you must now be introduced. It may be that Paul met him when Paul was sick, for the man was a physician, and could be of great service to him in his affliction. This new companion kept notes and afterwards wrote the "Acts of the Apostles" in which we learn most of the things we are telling you about. His name was Luke, called by Paul the "beloved Physician."

Over to Macedonia.

Paul told his vision to his brethren, and "immediately" Luke says, "we endeavored to go into Macedonia, assuredly gathering that the Lord had called us for to preach the Gospel unto them."

They sailed from Troas "with a straight course" across to Samothracia and "the next day to Neapolis; and from thence to Philippi, the chief city of that part of Macedonia."

LESSON 30 AT PHILIPPI

"The Gospel is the fulfillment of all hopes, the perfection of all philosophy, the interpreter of all revelations, and a key to all seeming contradictions of truth in the physical and moral world."

By the River Side.

Near the city of Philippi flowed the river Gaggitas. On its banks just "out of the city" was built a plain enclosure probably open at the top, in which a few people met to worship the Lord.

There was no synagogue in Philippi; and the few Jews who were there went to this place "by the river side" to offer their prayers, and to read the law. Most of those who did so were women.

When the first Sabbath day came after the elders had been in Philippi several days, they went to this place of worship, "sat down, and spake unto the women who resorted thither."

Gospel Preached.

No doubt evil minded men accused the missionaries in those days of trying to lead the women astray, just as enemies accuse the elders of the Church today. But lies and false accusations could not keep Paul and his associates from doing their duty. To these women, they preached the Gospel of Jesus Christ, and told them the story of His life. His cruel death and His glorious resurrection.

LYDIA

First in Europe to Accept Gospel.

In the group that listened to the wonderful message was "a certain woman named Lydia," who lived in Thyatira, but who was then in Philippi attending to her business connected with the dyeing trade. She sold purple dyes used by the rich and the nobility. The Lord gave her a testimony of the truth as Paul explained it, and she applied for baptism. She and "her household" were admitted into membership that day. If Lydia was the first one baptized, then she has the distinction of being the first person in Europe to accept Christianity. Whether "her household" means she had children, or whether it refers to her servants or to both we do not know, but they became the nuclueus of a thriving branch of the Church in that city, and in Lydia's home town as well.

After baptism, Lydia invited the missionaries to her home, saying, "If ye have judged me to be faithful to the Lord, come into my house, and abide there."

THE DAMSEL WITH THE SPIRIT OF DIVINATION

Evil Spirit Rebuked.

One day when the elders were going out to the place of prayer, they met an unfortunate woman who caused them no little annoyance. She was a damsel who seemed to be "possessed by some spirit of divination" which her masters (for she had more than one) used for making money. When she would meet the elders, she would cry out:

"These men are the servants of the most high God, which show unto us the way of salvation."

After she had done this on several different days, Paul became "grieved," not particularly because of what she said, but because he knew the evil spirit was tormenting her. So he turned to her one day, and said to the evil spirits:

"I command thee in the name of Jesus Christ to come out of her," and immediately she was healed.

Effect.

When her masters realized that their female slave had been cured, and that the hope of their gains was gone, they became very angry. "They caught Paul and Silas, and drew them into the court unto the rulers." But they were shrewd enough not to tell the magistrates the real reason why Paul and Silas had been brought there. They didn't say "these men cured our slave, and we cannot any longer fool the people for money." No, they accused them of breaking the Roman law by introducing "customs" and beliefs which it was unlawful for Romans to observe.

When the mob cried out "That is so," the magistrates gave the elders no opportunity to defend themselves, but condemned them to be taken out and beaten.

SCOURGED AND IMPRISONED

The "Inner Prison."

With their hands tied, and their backs bared to the whip, the elders were beaten "with many stripes." Bleeding and faint they were then taken to the prison. As the jailor received them, he was ordered to "keep them safely." Hearing this order and thinking the prisoners must be wicked men indeed, the jailor took them and "thrust them into the inner prison." The inner prison of a Roman jail was a dark, damp, gloomy dungeon. One writer calls it a "pestilential cell, damp and cold, from which the light was excluded, and where the chains rusted on the limbs of the prisoners." But not content with shutting the elders up in such a gloomy hole, "the jailor made their feet fast in the stocks." In fastening only their feet, however, he showed a little mercy for there were holes in the stock for the wrists and for the neck also.

Happiness in Gloom.

With their backs sore and bleeding, their bodies chilled by the cold and dampness, their legs cramped and aching, hungry and sleepless and surrounded by the blackness of midnight, Paul and Silas who knew they were suffering for the sake of the true Gospel, could rejoice and praise the Lord. This they did at midnight by praying and singing "praises unto God." Their voices rang out through the prison cells; and prisoners, hard hearted and sinful, listened in surprise to the first Christian hymn they had ever heard. The power of the Lord manifested itself not only in the hearts of His true servants, but in the entire prison and the town as well; for "suddenly there was a great earthquake, so that the foundations of the prison were shaken." All the bolts and bars at the doors fell from their sockets and the doors of the prison flew open, and "every one's bands were loosed," but not a prisoner tried to escape.

The Jailor's Fear.

Aroused from his sleep by the commotion and earthquake, the jailor hurried to the prison only to find the doors wide open. Remembering his injunction to "keep the prisoners safely," and knowing that he would forfeit his life if any had escaped, he drew his sword to take his own life, when Paul cried out:

"Do thyself no harm; for we are all here!"

"Then he [the jailor] called for a light and sprang in and came trembling and fell down before Paul and Silas."

PAUL AND SILAS IN PRISON AT PHILIPPI.
"Then he called for a light, and sprang in and came trembling and fell down before Paul and Silas."

HIS CONVERSION

An All-Important Question.

Perhaps he had heard what the damsel had said, that "These men are the servants of the most high God;" it may be that he had heard them preach, or at least had been told by others what they preached. Probably the earthquake itself had convinced him that these men not only were innocent, but were servants of God. At any rate, he cried out: "Sirs, what must I do to be saved?"

That is the question everybody should ask, and the answer, when truthfully given, everybody should obey.

The Answer.

Note the answer: "Believe in the Lord Jesus Christ, and thou shalt be saved, and thy house." Then the servants of the Lord explained what a true belief is, expounded the "word of the Lord," taught them faith and repentance and baptism; and when the keeper of the prison and his family said they believed the Gospel to be true, he led the elders out, washed their stripes, and was baptized that same night, "he and all his straightway."

Then he took them, not back to the dreary dungeon, but into his own house, and set meat before them. We are told that his heart was filled with rejoicing because he "believed in God with all his house."

By doing right he had opened the windows of his soul, and the sunshine of pure happiness had radiated through his entire being. He was experiencing the truth as expressed in the song:

"Doing good is a pleasure,
A joy beyond measure,
A blessing of duty and love."

Prisoners Released.

The earthquake or something else had put fear in the hearts of other men in that city, too, and among these were the magistrates who had sentenced, uncondemned, two innocent men to be beaten and imprisoned. Realizing their mistake they sent word early in the morning to the jailor to "Let those men go."

Paul Surprises the Jailor.

Pleased with the message, the keeper of the prison hurried to Paul and Silas crying: "The magistrates have sent to let you go: now therefore depart, and go in peace."

He was surprised to hear Paul coolly answer, "No, they have beaten us openly, uncondemned, being Romans, and have cast us into prison." Now they want us to go out privily so that people will think we are pestilent fellows who escaped from jail. "Nay verily, but let them come themselves and fetch us out."

Magistrates Humbled.

When the magistrates heard what Paul had said, and learned that Roman citizens had been scourged and thrust into prison without even a trial, they were very much afraid, for they realized that they might lose their offices. So they came, and led Paul and Silas out of the prison, and expressed a desire that the missionaries leave the city.

But the released prisoners had won a great victory; and while they did not flaunt it in the face of their persecutors, they took occasion to go to the house of Lydia, and meet all the Saints. Perhaps Paul reminded the Saints of the night in Jerusalem when Peter was released from prison and came to the house of Mary.

Whatever was said, we know that "when he had seen the brethren they comforted them and departed."

Luke remained to strengthen and build up the Church in Philippi, and Paul and his other companions went to Thessalonica.

LESSON 31 AT THESSALONICA AND BEREA

"A constant struggle, a ceaseless battle to bring success from inhospitable surroundings, is the price of all great achievements."

"To banish, imprison, plunder, starve, hang, and burn men for religion is not the Gospel of Christ, but the policy of the devil. Christ never used anything that looked like force but once, and that was to drive bad men out of the temple, not to drive them in."

It is easy enough to do right when in good company, but it is not easy to defend the right when the majority of the crowd are opposing it; and yet, that is the time to show true courage. The Prophet Joseph, for example, was reviled and persecuted for saying that he had received a vision, but he always remained true to his testimony. Though he "was hated and persecuted yet he said it was true that God had spoken to him, and

"*All the world could not make him think or believe otherwise*!"

Such is the courage and firmness everyone should have. When one knows what is right one should always have the courage to defend it even in the face of ridicule or punishment.

"It's easy enough to be virtuous
When nothing tempts you to stray;
When without or within
No voice of sin
Is luring your soul away;
But it's only a negative virtue
Until it is tried by fire:
And the soul that is worth
The praises of earth
Is the soul that resists desire."

In the matter of courage to preach the Gospel in the face of bitter persecution, the missionaries at Thessalonica and Berea proved themselves true heroes.

After the cruel treatment Paul had received in Philippi, he was not in a condition to endure long travel, and hardship; yet he and his companions traveled over one hundred miles before they reached Thessalonica.

This city, the capital of Macedonia, towards which Paul had been directing his course ever since he left Troas, was an important trading center. "Indeed, in all Greece," "if we except Corinth, there is no harbor with a finer situation; the anchorage is of the best; the roadstead is as smooth as a lake, while the neighboring valleys give access to highways leading into Epirus and upper Macedonia."[80]

How Named.

At one time the city was called Therma; but in the days of Alexander the Great, it was named Thessalonica for Alexander's sister, Thessalonica, the wife of one of Alexander's generals.

This name, slightly shortened clings to the city today. It is now called Saloniki and is one of the centers of the great war that is, at the present time,[81] wasting all Europe. In importance it is the second city in European Turkey.

Worn in Body; Fresh in Spirit.

Tired and worn and penniless, Paul entered this great city. Tired and worn in body, but fresh and vigorous as ever in spirit, he took immediate steps to give to the people the glorious message of the Gospel of the Redeemer.

In the Synagogue.

The first meeting was probably held in "the synagogue," for Thessalonica was then, and has been since, a strong Jewish center. For three successive weeks, Paul and Silas "reasoned with them out of the scriptures; opening and alleging that Christ must needs have suffered and risen again from the dead; and that this same Jesus, whom, he said, 'I preach unto you,' is Christ."

Nor was it only in the synagogue that these earnest missionaries proclaimed their message, but in the street and in the workshop.

With Jason.

Paul and Silas lodged with a man named Jason, where Paul worked at the trade he had learned in Tarsus. Paul says himself that he "labored night and day, that he might not be burdensome to any of them."[82] Thus "late at night, when the sun had long set on the incessant spiritual labors of the day, the apostle might be seen by lamplight laboring at the rough haircloth, that he might be chargeable to none."

Aided by the Saints.

---

[80] Touard
[81] 1915
[82] I Thess. 11:9.

We can well imagine that he was frequently interrupted in this work by men and women who would seek for more light on the doctrines of the Gospel. The result was that Paul made scarcely enough money to pay for his food and clothing; and if the good Saints in Philippi had not sent him relief, he and Silas would perhaps have been in actual want.

Not many Jews believed, so Paul and his companion turned to the Gentiles, many of whom believed, "of the devout Greeks a great multitude, and of the chief women not a few."

THE STORM GATHERS

A Mob.

But when the unbelieving Jews saw great numbers accepting this new Gospel, they became very jealous and angry. They went among a low, ignorant class of the citizens, "certain lewd fellows of the baser sort," and told them that these Christians are setting the whole world in an uproar, and ought to be driven out of the town. So they gathered a mob, and surrounded the house of Jason where the elders lodged.

Missionaries Warned.

But, fortunately, Paul and Silas were not in, and could not be found. Perhaps some friend, or it may be the Spirit of the Lord, had warned the Lord's servants not to go home just at that time. Not finding the elders, the mob dragged Jason and some other brethren before the rulers of the city and said:

Jason Seized.

"Those Christians that have turned the world upside down have come hither also;

"Whom Jason hath received; and these all do contrary to the decrees of Caesar, saying that there is another king, one Jesus."

How easy it is sometimes to prevert the truth into a lie!

Paul and Companions Escape.

Jason and his friends had to give "security;" (by which is probably meant that they had to deposit money as assurance that they would do nothing against the government), after which they were permitted to go free.

But the mob was still bitter against Paul and Silas who were advised by the brethren to leave immediately. This they did by night, traveling fifty-one miles to Berea.

AT BEREA

Many Accept Gospel.

Persecution and suffering could no more stop these inspired workers from preaching the Gospel than it could stop them from breathing; so as soon as they arrived at Berea, "they went into the synagogue of the Jews." The Jews here were more noble than those in Thessalonica, and would reason from the scripture, which was the Old Testament, kept in sacred rolls in the synagogue. So we conclude that the Bereans, not only listened attentively to what the missionaries told them but searched the scriptures to see if what they said was in harmony with the Law. When they found that it was, many believed, "also of honorable women who were Greeks, and of men not a few."

THE STORMS FOLLOWS THEM

As the Jews had gone once before from Iconium to Lystra, so they came now from Thessalonica to Berea, "like hunters upon their prey," and "stirred up the people."

Silas and Timothy Remain.

But the seeds of truth had taken root in the rich soil, and while the storm of persecution threatened to deluge Paul, it served only to strengthen and vitalize the Gospel field.

Paul Escapes.

Leaving Silas and Timothy to continue the work, to bless and encourage the Saints, Paul became once more a fugitive and was conducted by some of the brethren to the sea. From some point on the coast he embarked for Athens.

LESSON 32 AT ATHENS AND CORINTH

"Sometimes a noble failure serves the world as faithfully as a distinguished success."
"Life has no blessing like a prudent friend."

Loneliness.

Perhaps few if any of the young folks who read these lessons have ever been alone, even for a short time, in a strange city; but it may be that some of your fathers or brothers have, if so, you may learn by asking just how lonesome one can feel when one is in a large crowd, in a strange city, and out of sympathy with the people around him. To be

"Amid the crowd, the hum, the shock of men,
To hear, to see, to feel and to possess,
And roam along the world's tired denizen,
With none to bless us, none whom we can bless;
This is to be alone; this, this is solitude."

Such must have been Paul's condition after he said goodby to his brethren, and walked through the streets of Athens alone.

This loneliness impressed him so deeply that he afterwards wrote to the Thessalonians that he "was left in Athens alone."[83] He had sent a command back to Berea for "Silas and Timothy to come to him with all speed;" but until they came, he was the only Christian in the great pagan city.

Statues and Deities.

As Paul walked through the streets of Athens, he saw many statues and memorials built in honor of men and mystical gods. Some of these were the statues of the great men of Athens, "such as Solon the lawgiver, Conon the admiral, Demosthenes the orator." Among her defied heroes were Hercules, Mercury, Apollo, Neptune, Jupiter, Minerva, and many others, and in one place, in the center of all these was an altar to the "Twelve Gods." "There were more statues in Athens than in all the rest of Greece. It has been said as almost a truth that it was easier to find a god in Athens than a man."[84] There were

---

[83] I Thess. 3:1.
[84] Weed.

altars erected also to Fame, to Modesty, to Energy, to Persuasion, and to Pity, and Paul saw one inscription,

"To the Unknown God."

The Market Place.

In the city was a common meeting place called the Agora. Here the Athenians gathered to talk about and discuss the questions of the day. Idlers and professed philosophers mingled together eager to hear anything new. While Paul was waiting for his companions, he visited this gathering place daily, and conversed with those whom he met. From him the crowd heard, for the first time, about Jesus and the resurrection.

He also attended the service in the synagogue, and disputed with the Jews.

Interest Awakened.

So Paul, though lonely and discouraged, and perhaps gloomy because of the ignorance and wickedness he saw around him, "began to stir the city" because of the message he announced. The Athenians and strangers, too, began to get curious; for some of them, Luke tells us "spent their time in nothing else, but either to tell, or to hear some new thing."

Then certain philosophers began to hear about him, and took notice of him. Some said,

"What will this base fellow say?"

And others,

"He seemeth to be a setter forth of strange gods; because he preacheth unto them Jesus and the resurrection."

Mars' Hill.

On the top of the hill of Areopagus was a platform which was reached by a flight of stone steps leading immediately from the Agora. On this had sat the leading judges who had, for time immemorial, decided important questions of religion, or passed sentence on the greatest criminals. Because Mars was supposed to have had his trial there, it was called "Mars' Hill:" On the brow of this hill was built the temple of Mars.

To this important and memorable spot, the philosophers led the Apostle, saying,

"May we know what this new doctrine whereof thou speakest is? For thou bringest certain strange things to our ears; we would know, therefore, what these things mean."

A Memorable Address.

Paul accepted the invitation, and delivered one of the most memorable addresses in the world. You will notice, however, that he does not even mention the name of Christ, but tries to influence his hearers A by leading them from what they were interested in to that in which he wanted them to be interested.[85]

Interrupted.

As soon as Paul mentioned the resurrection of the dead, he was interrupted. Some broke out into laughter and made light of his remark. Others were more courteous, and said, as they withdrew from him, "We will hear thee again on this matter."

Converted Dionysius.

Paul must have felt almost crushed with the thought that his sermon had been an utter failure; but he had done his duty and the seeds of truth had been sown. They bore fruit in the conversion of Dionysius, a member of the court of the Areopagus, and of a woman whose name was Damaris, and "others with them."

After remaining a short time, "he left Athens as he had lived in it, a despised and lonely man." Yet that short visit, and that interrupted speech, characterized, as both were, by a sincere desire to call the erring and wicked to repentance, have made Paul more famous than any of the philosophers, so wise in their own conceit, who mocked and spurned him.

AT THE CLOSE OF THE SECOND MISSION

Alone in Corinth.

It is probable that Timothy joined Paul in Athens; but if so, he returned immediately to the churches in Macedonia. Thus it was that Paul sailed from Athens alone, and having landed at the seaport of Cenchrea, walked eighteen miles to Corinth. Here he found many Greeks and Jews. There were crowds also of strangers who came to see the great games and races for which Corinth was noted. Corinth, at that time, was a great commercial center, and merchantmen and other traders from far and near made up its population. If Athens was a learned city, Corinth was a wealthy and wicked one. So Paul's loneliness here must have been just as keen as it was in Athens. Indeed, he says himself that he went there "in weakness and in fear and in much trembling."[86]

---

[85] Read and explain sermon Acts 17:22-31.

[86] I Cor. 2:3.

Aquila and Priscilla.

Just about that time a Roman emperor named Claudius issued a decree that all Jews should be banished from Rome. Among those who had to leave were a man named Aquila and his wife Priscilla. Whether they were Christians before they came to Corinth is not known. At any rate, they were among the first friends Paul met in that city. It may be that they became acquainted because Aquila and Paul had the same trade. At any rate, Paul lived with them, and (if they were not Christians before) converted them to the Gospel, to which they remained staunch and true. These friends were a help to Paul in furnishing him employment, but in a greater way by proving to be true friends indeed.

In the Synagogue.

Every Sabbath day, these three friends and fellow-laborers would lay aside their unfinished tents, and go to the synagogue to worship the Lord. Paul, as usual, would speak to his countrymen and to the converted Greeks, and proclaim to them the glorious message of the risen Redeemer. He would reason with them from the scripture, and persuade them to become Christians.

Timothy and Silas Join Paul.

For some time, he seems to have been less energetic than usual. He was more discouraged than enthusiastic. But, just at that period, he was joined by his two dear friends, Timothy and Silas. Their coming gave him new heart, or as Luke says, "he was pressed in the spirit, and testified to the Jews that Jesus was the Christ." Judging from the strength Paul received from the companionship of these friends, he realized that,

"A true friend is the gift of God, and He only who made hearts can unite them."

Jews Reject Truth.

But the more boldly and earnestly Paul preached, the more bitterly those unconverted Jews opposed him. Finally, when they blasphemed the name of God, and refused to accept the truth, Paul "shook his raiment," and said, "Your blood be upon your own heads; I am clean; from henceforth I will go unto the Gentiles."

Crispus Converted.

But many were converted, and among these was—Crispus, the chief ruler of the synagogue—"he and all his house." His conversion, with the crowds of Corinthians who were baptized also, only made the Jews more bitter than ever; and they began to threaten Paul.

Comfort.

About this time Paul wrote his second letter to the Thessalonians. In it he asks, especially, for their prayers that he might be delivered from the wicked men around him. "Pray for us, brethren," he pleads, "that the word of the Lord may be preached freely; and that we may be delivered from unreasonable and wicked men: for all have not faith."[87]

And Paul prayed, too, and he received a direct answer from the Lord, who said: "Be not afraid, but speak, and hold not thy peace:

"For I am with thee, and no man shall set on thee to hurt thee: for I have much people in this city."

In the House of Justus.

When Paul left the synagogue, he held meetings in a house that "joined hard to the synagogue;" that is, it was perhaps next to it. Here Paul and his two companions continued preaching. This so exasperated the Jews that they concluded to try to get Paul either expelled or punished.

Before Gallio.

Now it so happened that just at that time a new governor was appointed over Achaia. His name was Gallio, and he was known as a very "kind and gentle man." Thinking he would be easily influenced, the Jews had Paul arrested, and dragged him before the "judgment seat," saying falsely, "This fellow persuadeth men to worship God contrary to the law."

Paul arose, or beckoned some way that he desired to answer the charge; but Gallio stopped him, and addressing the Jews, said:

"If it were a matter of wrong or wicked lewdness, O ye Jews, reason would that I should bear with you; but if it be a question of words and names, and of your law, look ye to it; for I will be no judge of such matters."

And he drove them from his presence.

Persecutors Punished.

So Paul was not harmed, just as the Lord promised. But the Jews were; for the Greeks took their leader and whipped him even before the "judgment seat."

---

[87] II Thes. 3:1-2.

Paul remained in Corinth one year and a half, and established there a strong church.

Then, as the time for the Passover at Jerusalem was drawing near, he bade goodby to the Saints; and taking Aquila and Priscilla, Silas and Timothy, his faithful friends and companions, he set sail for Ephesus, thence to Caesarea, and Jerusalem.

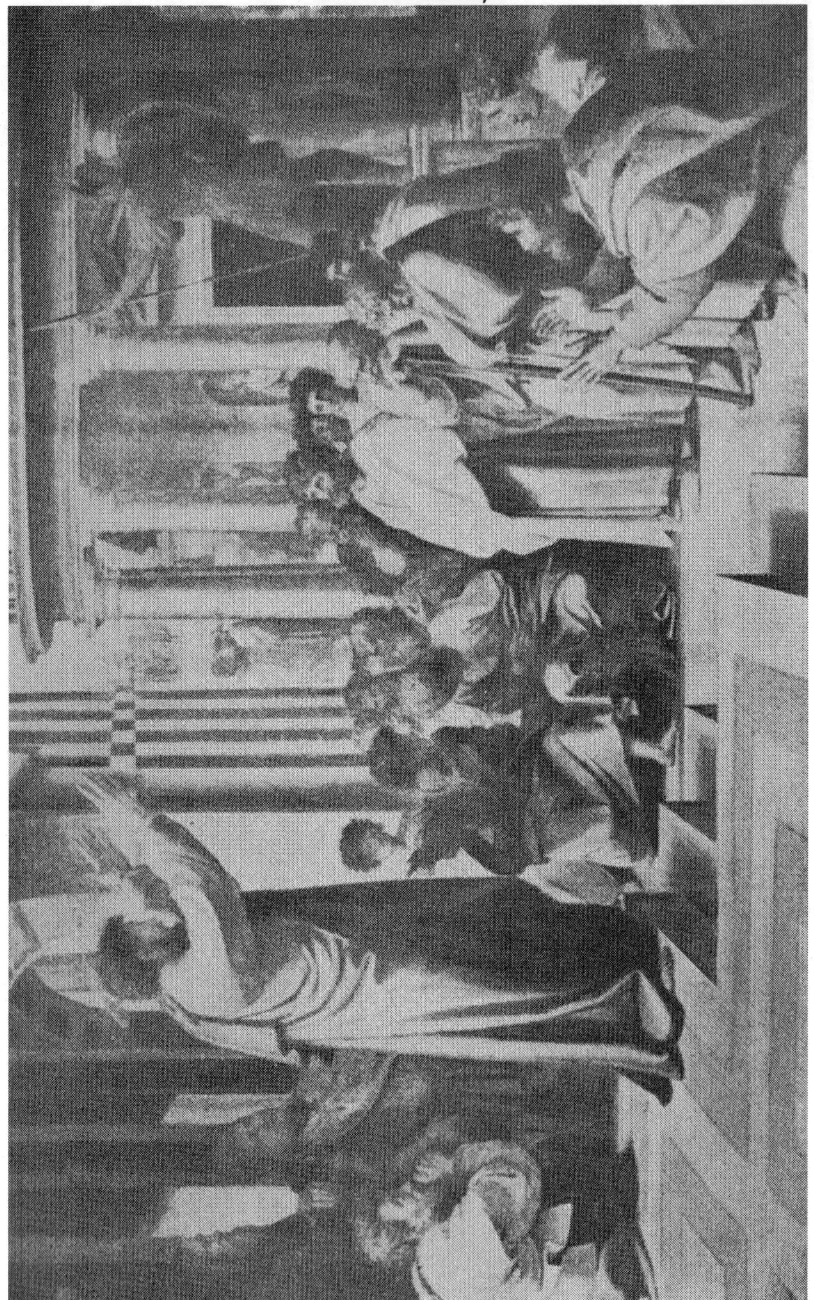

ST. PAUL AT ATHENS.

"And when they heard of the resurrection of the dead, some mocked and others said, we will hear thee again on this matter."

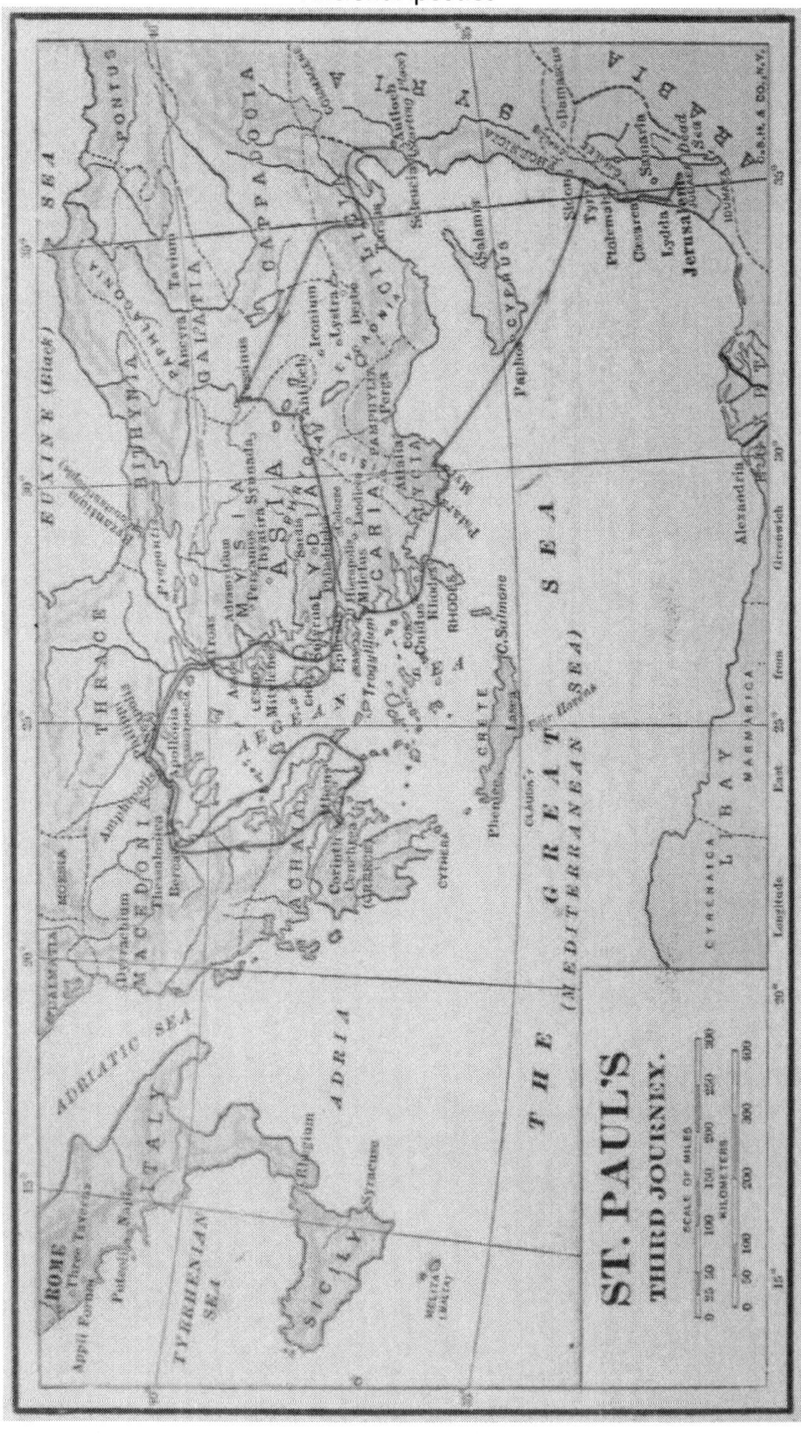
ST. PAUL'S
THIRD JOURNEY.

LESSON 33 PAUL'S THIRD MISSIONARY JOURNEY FROM ANTIOCH TO EPHESUS

"No man taketh this honor unto himself but he that is called of God as was Aaron."

A Promise.

When Paul stopped off at Ephesus on his way to Jerusalem, as mentioned in the previous lesson, the Jews to whom he preached asked him "to tarry a longer time with them." Not being able to do so, he promised them to "return again if God will." This promise, as we shall see, Paul literally fulfilled.

Salutes the Church.

Whether he arrived in Jerusalem in time to attend the Passover we do not know. In fact we are led to infer that he did not, for all that we know of this visit is that he "saluted the church," and went down to Antioch.

Beginning of Third Journey.

After spending some time with the important church in Antioch, Paul started on his third missionary journey. Just what course he followed, it is difficult to determine; but since Luke tells us that he went "over all the country of Galatia and Phrygia in order," we may safely conclude that he visited his old home in Tarsus, as well as the cities of Derbe, Lystra, Iconium, and possibly Antioch in Pisidia. The good people in Galatia also would again have the pleasure of meeting the apostle who first preached to them the Gospel, and to whom they had so kindly administered in affliction.

Neither do we know of a certainty who were his companions. Timotheus, undoubtedly, was one who accompanied him on the whole of his journey.

APOLLOS

An Eloquent Preacher.

While Paul and Timothy are visiting the churches in Galatia and Phrygia, let us hasten ahead of them to Ephesus; for there is a man there whose acquaintance we should make. His name is Apollos and he came from Alexandria. He was, undoubtedly, one of the most eloquent preachers of the Gospel in that day.

But when he first came to Ephesus, he "knew only the baptism of John." He had accepted the message of John the Baptist, but he had not heard the Gospel as it had been taught by Jesus and His disciples. He seemed to have been ignorant of the mission of the Holy Ghost.

With him were twelve other men who held the same incomplete belief.

New Light.

Believing they had the truth, these men went to the same synagogue in which Paul had preached when the Jews asked him to tarry longer, and Apollos spoke to the people. In the congregation sat Aquila and Priscilla. These good Christians perceived at once that Apollos did not understand the Gospel; so, they invited him home with them and "expounded unto him the way of God more perfectly."

Shortly after this, Apollos left Ephesus for Corinth, taking with him a letter of recommendation from the Saints in Ephesus.

THE HOLY GHOST GIVEN

Thus it was that when Paul arrived in Ephesus he met the twelve men who had been taught the Gospel as Apollos had known it. When they told Paul that they believed the Gospel, he asked them, "Have ye received the Holy Ghost since ye believed?"

"We have not so much as heard whether there be any Holy Ghost," they answered.

"Unto what then were ye baptized?" asked Paul.

"Unto John's baptism," they replied.

"John verily baptized with the baptism of repentance," said Paul, "saying unto the people, that they should believe on Him which should come after him that is, on Christ Jesus."

They were then baptized by the proper authority, in the name of the Lord Jesus. Paul then "laid his hands upon them" and "the Holy Ghost came on them; and they spoke with tongues, and prophesied."

Three Months in the Synagogue.

For three months Paul continued to preach in the synagogue, "disputing and persuading the things concerning the Kingdom of God." During this time, he worked at his trade supporting himself "with his hands." Daily the Church grew in strength, and daily its enemies became so bitter in their opposition that Paul left the synagogue, and held his meetings in a schoolhouse where taught a man named Tyrannus.

Two Years at Ephesus.

In this place, Paul labored for two years, a period in his life marked by wonderful manifestations from the Lord. Sick people were healed by the power of faith in most miraculous ways. Sometimes when Paul could not visit in person those afflicted, they would be healed by simply touching a handkerchief or an apron he had worn. Thus "the name of the Lord Jesus was magnified."

MEN WHO ACTED WITHOUT AUTHORITY

Sons of Sceva.

Among those who witnessed these miracles were some vagabond Jews who made a living by deceiving the people by pretending to be magicians. When they saw Paul heal the sick in the name of Jesus, they thought they could do the same, and thus make a great deal of money. So one day these seven men who were sons of Sceva, meeting a man who was afflicted with an evil spirit, said, "We adjure you by Jesus whom Paul preacheth," to come out of him.

"Jesus I know," said the evil spirit, "and Paul I know, but who are ye?" And the man leaped on them, and overcame them, so that they fled out of the house naked and wounded.

A Big Bonfire.

The treatment that these seven men received through their hypocrisy, soon spread over the city. Many who had practiced such arts as the sons of Sceva had, brought all their books of magic and made a bonfire of them. Paul saw burned that day about $10,000 worth of books and papers.

Annual Festival.

Every year in Ephesus, in the month of May, there was held a great festival in honor of the Goddess Diana. Rich men came from all parts of Asia, and "paid vast sums of money for the entertainment of the people. The entertainments were of different kinds. In the theatre were concerts and shows; in the hippodrome horse-racing; in the stadium gymnastic games of running, leaping and wrestling. There were noisy scenes through the day and night. In every hour of the day there were gay processions to the temple, following the bleating animals crowned with garland, being led to sacrifice. Idlers and drunkards could be seen almost everywhere at any time. * * * The shops and bazaars were filled with all the attractive things of those days which parents and friends would buy themselves and those left in distant homes. The special mementos would be little models of Diana and her shrine. The poorest of purchasers would buy those made of wood; others those of silver; and the wealthy those of gold."[88]

A Loss of Trade.

[88] Weed

Paul, no doubt, had told the Ephesians as he had the Athenians, that God is not made of wood or of silver, or of gold, "neither graven by art of man's devise." These were hundreds and thousands of people who believed Paul and worshiped the true God. Consequently, at this annual feast, there were not so many images of Diana bought as there had been at other festivals.

A MOB GATHERS

Demetrius

Demetrius, a sliversmoth, who made silver shrines for Diana, became very much agitated when he saw his trade interfered with. He called together all his workmen and said:

"Sirs, ye know by this craft we have our wealth. Moreover ye see and hear, that not alone at Ephesus but almost throughout all Asia, this Paul hath persuaded and turned away much people, saying that they be no gods, which are made with hands."

He continued to speak to them until they became thoroughly aroused and cried out, "Great is Diana of the Ephesians."

Paul's Companions Seized.

Soon the whole city became in confusion. A mob gathered, and tried to find Paul. Failing in this, they caught Gaius and Aristarchus, two of Paul's companions, and rushed them into the theatre.

Paul was kept in safety by his friends who refused to let him enter the theatre, although he insisted on doing so.

A Howling Mob.

A Jew named Alexander tried to speak to the mob, but they would not listen, and continued to howl for two hours, "Great is Diana of the Ephesians, Great is Diana of the Ephesians."

When they had worn themselves out, the town clerk arose and told them they had better go home and be quiet, or the Romans might "call them in question for this day's uproar." He said, too, that if Demetrius had any case against Paul, he could have Paul arrested and taken into court.

As half the people, as is the case of all mobs, did not know why they had come, they began to move out of the theatre. "The stone seats were gradually emptied, the uproar ceased and the rioters dispersed to their various occupations and amusements."

As Paul had already made preparations to go into Macedonia, he called the disciples to him, and after embracing them, left Ephesus so far as we know, forever. Later, however, as we shall learn in the next lesson, he met some of the Elders and Saints from Ephesus.

LESSON 34 THIRD MISSIONARY JOURNEY—(Continued)

Paul's farewell visit to churches he had established

During the next nine or ten months—from the summer, A. D., 57, to the spring, A. D., 58—following Paul's affectionate farewell to the disciples at Ephesus, we know very little of his travels. From the epistles that he wrote during this period, we learn most of what is known about his labors and duties "over those parts" in Macedonia.

He first went to Troas, where he expected to meet Titus whom he had sent to Corinth. Here, he says, "I had no rest in my spirit, because I found not Titus, my brother."[89]

Worrying over the reports he had heard about the evil conditions in the Corinthian church, he left Troas for Philippi.

A Joyous Welcome.

Here he met some of his most beloved Saints; for the Philippian converts, though among the poorest, financially, were among the most faithful of all the churches. Paul had accepted their assistance when he had refused help from other sources. This is one church which Paul did not reprove. What a joyous welcome these faithful Saints must have given the Apostle! How their hearts would rejoice as they retold their experiences when Paul and Timothy and Silas first preached to the women by the river side. Lydia and the jailor and a host of other faithful members would all be there to recall the arrest, the whipping, the imprisonment, the stocks, the midnight hymns, the earthquake, the authorities' fears and all the other wonderful experiences of that first visit to Philippi!

Paul Depressed.

Yet amidst all this welcome Paul says his "flesh had no rest; without were fightings, within were fears; until God who comforts them that are cast down, comforted me by the coming of Titus."[90]

Second Epistle to Corinthians.

Titus told him that the members of the Church in Corinth who had been doing wrong had been excommunicated, and that many of the saints were doing better. Hearing this, Paul wrote another letter to

---

[89] II Cor. 2:13.

[90] II Cor. 7:6

them, (the second Epistle to the Corinthians) and sent Titus back with it.

Offerings.

Titus seems to have been one of the chief men in collecting contributions for the relief of the poor in Judea. When he returned to Corinth, he continued to make collections for Paul to take to Jerusalem in the near future.[91]

The next we hear of Paul, he is in Corinth. While there he hears that the Galatians were saying that he was not an apostle because Jesus had not chosen him as one of the Twelve. So he wrote a letter to the Galatians in which he says,

Galatians Reproved.

"I marvel that ye are so soon removed from him that called you unto the grace of Christ unto another Gospel."

Then he warns them against accepting any other Gospel, for if anyone preach any other Gospel, "let him be accursed."

Here he also wrote his epistle to the Romans.

Retraces Steps.

Paul prepared to go to Palestine direct from Corinth, but he heard of a plot to take his life. To frustrate this, he retraced his steps through Macedonia. When the company again reached Philippi, Timothy and several others went ahead to Troas. Paul and Luke remained for a short time and then rejoined the company at Troas.

A LONG AND MEMORABLE MEETING

When Sunday came, all the disciples "came together to break bread," and Paul preached to them his farewell sermon. As he was to leave them in the morning, they persuaded him to continue his speech until midnight, which he did.

The meeting was held in an upper room, the windows of which were all thrown open so the congregation could enjoy the cool of the evening.

Eutychus Falls.

Sitting in one of the windows was a young man named Eutychus who listened to the sermon as long as he could, and then fell asleep. As Paul continued to preach, Eutychus continued to nod, until finally he became overbalanced and fell into the courtyard below. No doubt a

[91] II Cor. 8.

woman's scream first interrupted the sermon. The people sprang to their feet, and rushed below, and picked the young man up for dead.

Restored.

Paul, too, went down, and embracing the boy, said,

"Trouble not yourselves for his life is in him."

Thankful that the young man was restored, the people returned to the room, and Paul preached to them until morning.

Paul's companions went by ship to Assos, but he preferred to walk the twenty miles alone.

At Assos he went abroad the ship and sailed to Mitylene, thence to Chios, and the next day to Samos, about a mile from which they tarried at Trogyllium.

At Miletus.

On the next day, Paul sailed past Ephesus, thinking that he would not have time to visit the Saints there, for he wanted to be in Jerusalem on the day of Pentecost. But when he reached Miletus, a few miles from Ephesus, he sent word over to the Elders of the Church to come to him. This they did with all gladness, and listened with intense interest to his address to them.[92]

"And when he had thus spoken, he kneeled down and prayed with them all."

That little company of Christians assembled in an obscure place on the seashore presents to our minds one of the most beautiful pictures of the world, and their farewell greeting one of the most impressive and pathetic.

A Sad Farewell.

When the beloved apostle was about to leave them, "they all wept sore, and fell on Paul's neck, and kissed him; sorrowing most of all for the words which he spake." It seemed that they just could not bear to have him leave them. They clung to him even when he went aboard the ship, and it was with difficulty that his companions drew Paul from them.

A similar scene was enacted at Tyre where the company remained seven days. While Paul was visiting and comforting the Saints here, they entreated him not to go up to Jerusalem, because his life would be in danger. But Paul could not be persuaded.

When the time came to say "goodby," the men, women and children all went with Paul and his company down to the shore. Here

---

[92] See Acts 20:17-35

they all kneeled down and prayed, and bade farewell "one of another." Then Paul and his companions entered the ship, and the sorrowing Saints returned slowly to their homes.

AT CAESAREA

At Caesarea the missionaries were entertained by Philip, the evangelist, one of the seven chosen deacons.

A Prophecy.

While they were there, Agabus, a prophet came down from Jerusalem and after greeting them all, took Paul's girdle, and bound his own hands and feet, saying,

"Thus sayeth the Holy Ghost, so shall the Jews at Jerusalem bind the man that owneth this girdle, and shall deliver him into the hands of the Gentiles."

Hearing this prophecy, Luke and all Paul's company pleaded with him not to go to Jerusalem. But Paul answered,

Ready to Die.

"What mean ye to weep and to break my heart? for I am ready not to be bound only, but also to die at Jerusalem for the name of the Lord Jesus."

"All right," said his friends, "The will of the Lord be done."

From Caesarea, they traveled by carriage to Jerusalem, where the brethren received them gladly.

LESSON 35 EXCITING EXPERIENCES IN JERUSALEM

"In the huge mass of evil as it rolls and swells, there is ever some good working toward deliverance and triumph."

At Headquarters.

At Jerusalem, Paul and his companions met with the Church and undoubtedly gave the money that had been given by the Gentile churches for the benefit of the poor in Judea. At the advice of James, the brother of the Lord, who was then presiding over the Church in Jerusalem, Paul shaved his head, and did certain other things to show the Jews that he was willing to observe the Jewish laws.

Falsely Accused.

When he had been in Jerusalem about a week, he went to the temple to worship. There happened to be also in the temple, some men who had seen Paul in Asia with the Gentiles. Thinking that he had brought some of these Gentiles into the temple, they stirred up the people, seized Paul, and cried out, "Men of Israel, help; this is the man that teacheth all men everywhere against the people, and the law, and this place; and further brought Greeks also into the temple, and hath polluted this place."

Of course, this was not true, but it served to arouse the crowd, who dragged Paul out of the temple and shut the doors. In their rage they were about to kill Paul, which they would have done but for the timely interference of a Roman officer.

Stationed in the castle north of the temple was a guard of soldiers under command of an officer called the "Chief Captain."

Rescued From Death.

When somebody told the captain, whose name was Claudius Lysius, that there was trouble in the outer court of the temple, he hurried the soldiers down there just as the mob began to beat and trample Paul to death. The soldiers rescued Paul; but the captain thinking he was a desperate man, commanded him to be bound with chains.

"Who is this man, and what has he done?" Claudius asked of the angry Jews.

Some cried one thing and some another in such confusion that the chief captain could understand nothing; so he said to the soldiers, "Carry him to the castle."

On the Castle Steps.

As the soldiers bore Paul away, the mob, acting like wolves after their prey, followed, crying, "Away with him." Just as they were going up the steps into the castle, Paul speaking in Greek said to the chief captain, "May I speak unto thee?"

"Canst thou speak Greek?" answered the captain, "Aren't you that Egyptian who sometime ago made an uproar here and led out into the wilderness four thousand men that were murderers?"

"I am a Jew from Tarsus," answered Paul, "a city in Cilicia, a citizen of no mean city, I beseech thee let me speak unto the people."

Hoping to learn something about the cause of the uproar the chief captain gave his consent.

Paul turned to the people and beckoned for them to be quiet. Their yelling ceased, especially when they heard Paul speak in Hebrew, their own language.[93]

The Word "Gentiles."

The Jews listened to him quietly until he happened to mention the word "Gentiles," then they cried, "Away with such a fellow from the earth; for it is not fit that he should live."

In their anger, they took off their coats and threw dust in the air to show how they hated him.

Ordered Whipped.

Being still in doubt as to what Paul had done, the chief captain ordered him brought into the castle and whipped until Paul told why the Jews cried so against him. As they were binding him to beat him, Paul said to the centurion who stood by.

"Is it lawful for you to whip a man who is a Roman and uncondemned?"

When the centurion heard this, he hurried to the chief captain saying, "Take heed what thou doest; for this man is a Roman." Then the chief captain came and said to Paul,

"Tell me, art thou a Roman?"

"Yes," answered Paul.

"With a great sum obtained I this freedom," said Claudius.

"But I was a free born Roman," proudly answered Paul.

When they heard this, those who were going to torture him hurried away from him, and the chief captain, too, was troubled; for

---

[93] Read the entire speech as recorded in Acts 22:1-21.

he knew he had no right to put chains on a Roman citizen who had not had a fair trial.

BEFORE ANANIAS THE HIGH PRIEST

Next morning Paul was brought before Ananias the High Priest and the Council.

Paul Smitten.

"And Paul earnestly beholding the council said,

"Men and brethren, I have lived in all good conscience before God until this day."

At this Ananias became so enraged that he said to those who stood by Paul,

"Smite him on the mouth."

"God shall smite thee, thou whited wall," answered Paul with sudden anger. "Sittest thou to judge me after the law, and commandest me to be smitten contrary to the law?"

Temper Controlled.

Those who stood nearest Paul said, "Revilest thou God's High Priest?" Then Paul, getting control of his feelings answered,

"I did not know, brethren, that he was the High Priest; for it is written, Thou shalt not speak evil of the ruler of thy people."

Two Sects.

Paul then noticed that in the council were two parties, some Pharisees and some Sadducees; so by speaking wisely of the resurrection, he won the Pharisees on his side, who said,

"We find no evil in this man. It may be that an angel or a spirit has spoken to him."

This made the Sadducees angry, the two factions got to quarreling and became so angry at each other that the chief captain fearing that they would tear Paul to pieces, commanded the soldiers to take him back to the castle.

Divine Comfort.

On the next night while Paul was still in the castle, the Lord stood by him and said,

"Be of good cheer, Paul; for as thou hast testified of me in Jerusalem so must thou also bear witness at Rome."

A Plot to Kill.

On the following morning about forty of these angary Jews bound themselves together by an oath, swearing that they would neither eat nor drink until they had killed Paul. To accomplish this, they said to the chief Priests, "we have bound ourselves under a great oath that we will taste nothing until we have slain Paul. Now, you ask the chief captain to bring him down to you tomorrow, as though you would inquire something more; and we, as soon as he comes near us, will be ready to kill him."

But their plot became known to Paul's sister's son, who hastened to the castle, and told his uncle all about it. After hearing his nephew's story, Paul called one of the centurions, and said,

The Plot Frustrated.

"Take this young man to the chief captain; for he hath a certain thing to tell him." The centurion did as directed and said to the chief captain,

"Paul, the prisoner, called me to him, and asked me to bring this young man unto thee, who hath something to say unto thee."

"What is it thou hast to tell me?" asked the chief captain.

"The Jews have agreed to ask you to take Paul tomorrow into the Council, as though they would inquire somewhat of him more perfectly. But do not thou yield unto them; for there lie in wait for him about forty men, who have bound themselves together with an oath that they will neither eat nor drink till they have killed him."

The chief captain believed the young man and said to him.

"See thou tell no man that thou hast shewed these things to me." The chief captain then called two centurions saying,

"Make ready two hundred soldiers to go to Caesarea, and seventy horsemen, and two hundred spearmen. Tell them to be ready at nine o'clock tonight to take Paul safely unto Felix the governor."

Claudius Lysius then wrote a letter to Governor Felix explaining, briefly, why Paul was being sent to him.[94] He also sent word to Paul's accusers to go to the Governor and make their charges known.

When Paul, safe and sound, appeared before Felix, the Governor asked,

At Caesarea.

"What province are you from?"

"From Cilicia," Paul answered.

"I will hear thee," said Felix, "when thine accusers are also come."

---

[94] See Acts 23:25-30.

Paul was then put in Herod's judgment hall until his trial five days later.

In Confinement.

Thus had Paul's life within the short space of a few days been twice preserved from those who wanted to kill him. God had spoken to him, saying, "Be of good cheer," and although he was still a prisoner, there was peace in his soul for he knew he had done only what was right, and that God approved of his labors.

LESSON 36 TWO YEARS IN PRISON

"I have a conscience void of offense toward God and all men."—Joseph Smith.

BEFORE FELIX

Five days after Paul had been put in the Judgment Hall, the high priest Ananias and some of his elders came to Caesarea to appear against him. They brought with them a lawyer named Tertullus.

Felix, the Roman Governor, summoned the prisoner to appear before him to hear from the Jewish lawyer what things Paul had done. The hired lawyer began his speech by flattering Felix, to win his favor, and then charged Paul as follows:

Paul Falsely Accused.

"This man is a pestilent fellow, a mover of sedition among all the Jews throughout the world and a ringleader among the sect called Nazarenes. He has profaned the temple, and has done many other things for which he should be punished."

And the Jews all cried out,

"Yes, these things are true."

When they had spoken, Felix motioned with his hand for Paul to speak in his own defense, which he did by saying:

Paul's Defense.

"As I know that thou hast been of many years a judge over this people, I cheerfully answer for myself these charges of the Jews. Twelve days ago, I went up to Jerusalem to worship; but I deny that I disputed with any man, or that I stirred up the people, either in the synagogues, or in the city. Neither can they prove the charges they make against me.

"This, however, I do confess, that after the way which they call heresy, so worship I the God of my fathers, believing in the law and the prophets, and in the resurrection of the dead, both of the just and the unjust; and I try to live to have always a clear conscience void of offense toward God, and men."

Innocent but a Prisoner.

Paul spoke so earnestly and honestly that Felix was convinced he spoke the truth; and when he concluded, Felix knew he was innocent, but, for fear of displeasing the Jews, who, he could see, hated Paul, he told the officers to hold Paul a prisoner, but to give him his liberty, and to let his friends come to see him. So Ananias and Turtullus had to go back to Jerusalem without having seen Paul punished. They still hoped, however, to get him either scourged or killed.

Before Felix and Druscilla.

Several days later, Felix and his wife Druscilla, a Jewess, called Paul before them to hear more about this Christian doctrine. Unfortunately the governor and his wife had not lived a good life; so when Paul "reasoned of righteousness, temperance, and judgment to come upon sinners, Felix trembled, and answered,

"Go away for this time; when I find it again convenient to hear you, I will send for you."

Offered a Bribe.

Felix was not a just judge, yet he wanted to dismiss Paul; but he hoped to get some money for doing it. So he called the prisoner before him many times, and hinted that if Paul would give him money, he would free him; but Paul scorned the intimation to be bribed.

So for two years Paul was kept in prison; but during that time, he no doubt preached the Gospel to many of his friends, and perhaps to many strangers as well. When Felix was released as governor, "willing to show the Jews a pleasure, he left Paul bound."

BEFORE FESTUS

Another Wicked Scheme.

Felix was succeeded by Festus, who was a more just and honorable governor. Festus remained in Caesarea about three days, and went up to visit Jerusalem. Then the chief priests and others tried to poison his mind against Paul, and asked that he might be brought from Caesarea to Jerusalem to be tried. It was their wicked plan to waylay Paul and kill him.

But Festus answered, "This prisoner will be kept at Caesarea, and I will return there myself. Let some of your ablest men go down with me, and prove that this man is as wicked as you say."

Ten days later, in Caesarea, Festus sat on the judgment seat, and summoned Paul before him. They again accused Paul of many wicked things, but could prove none of them. Paul again answered for himself, saying,

Denies Charges.

"I have done no wrong against the law of the Jews, neither against the temple; nor against Caesar."

Festus, desiring to please the Jews, and not knowing that they desired to kill Paul, said,

"Are you willing to go up to Jerusalem, and there be judged of these things before me?"

"I am standing in a Roman court, where I ought to be judged; I have not wronged the Jews, as thou very well knowest; and no man shall deliver me unto them. I appeal unto Caesar."

Appeal to Caesar.

Paul, you remember, was a Roman citizen; and therefore, had the right under the law to be tried at Rome before Caesar, the emperor.

Festus, after conferring with his council, said to Paul.

"Hast thou appealed unto Caesar? Then unto Caesar shalt thou go."

So Paul was taken to prison to await a favorable opportunity to be sent to Rome.

BEFORE KING AGRIPPA

When Paul was blind just after his vision, the Lord said, "He is a chosen vessel unto me, to bear my name before the Gentiles and kings, and the children of Israel." Among the rulers to whom Paul preached the Gospel were King Agrippa and his sister Bernice. Agrippa, who ruled over part of the land on the east side of the river Jordan, paid Festus a visit; and the Governor took occasion to tell the King all about Paul, how he had been left a prisoner by Felix; how the Jews had accused him, but failed to prove their charges; how he refused to go to Jerusalem; and how finally he had appealed to Caesar.[95]

Said Agrippa, "Festus, I should like to hear this man myself."

"All right," said Festus, "tomorrow thou shalt hear him."

A Royal Assembly.

On the morrow, Agrippa and Bernice came with "great pomp;" which means, no doubt, that he dressed in his purple robes and she in her bright jewels, and attended with servants all dressed in gorgeous colors. It was a royal assemblage, and a royal occasion, but the most royal personage among them was the humble prisoner who appeared in chains to plead his innocence and the justice of his cause.

---

[95] Acts 25:13-22.

The King, looking at Paul, with more curiosity than contempt, said,

"Thou art permitted to speak for thyself."

Then Paul, addressing himself principally to Agrippa, delivered a most impressive address as follows:

An Impressive Address.

"I think myself happy, King Agrippa, that I shall answer for myself, before thee, of all the things charged against me by the Jews; because I know that thou dost know all about the customs and the questions which are among the Jews. I ask thee then, to hear me patiently.

"My manner of life from my youth, all the Jews know, for I lived among them; and if they would tell the truth, they would testify that after the most strict sect of our religion, I lived a Pharisee. And now I stand and am to be judged for the hope of the promise made of God unto our fathers; that promise unto which our twelve tribes, constantly serving God day and night, hope to come. For this hope, King Agrippa, I am accused of the Jews. Why should it be thought a thing which thou couldst not believe, that God should raise the dead?

"At one time, I verily thought myself, that I ought to do many things contrary to the name of Jesus of Nazareth; and this I did in Jerusalem: and many of the Saints I shut up in prison, having received authority from the chief priests; and even when they were put to death, I gave my voice against them.

"And I punished them oft in every synagogue, and compelled them to blaspheme; and being exceedingly mad against them, I persecuted them even unto strange cities. Whereupon as I went to Damascus with authority and commission from the chief priests, at midday, O King, I saw in the way a light from heaven, above the brightness of the sun, shining round about me and them who journeyed with me. And when we were all fallen to the earth, I heard a voice speaking unto me, saying, in the Hebrew tongue:

"'Saul, Saul, why persecutest thou me?'

"And I said, 'Who art thou. Lord?'

"And he answered, 'I am Jesus whom thou persecutest, But rise, and stand upon thy feet: for I have appeared unto thee for this purpose, to make thee a minister and a witness both of these things which thou hast seen, and of those things in which I will appear unto thee; delivering thee from the people, and from the Gentiles, unto whom now I send thee, to open their eyes, and to turn them from darkness to light, and from the power of Satan unto God, that they may receive forgiveness of sins, and inheritance among them who are sanctified by faith that is in me.'

"Whereupon, O King Agrippa, I was not disobedient unto the heavenly vision: but explained first unto them of Damascus, and at Jerusalem, and throughout all the coasts of Judea, and then to the Gentiles, that they should repent and turn to God, and to works meet for repentance.

"For these causes the Jews caught me in the temple, and went about to kill me.

"Having therefore obtained help of God, I continue unto this day, witnessing both to small and great, saying none other things than those which the prophets and Moses did say should come, that Christ should suffer, and that he should be the first to rise from the dead, and should show light unto the people, and to the Gentiles."

An Interruption.

Just at this point in his address, Paul was interrupted by Festus, who cried,

"Paul, thou art beside thyself; much learning doth make thee mad!"

But Paul said, "I am not mad, most noble Festus; but speak forth the words of truth and soberness.

"The king knoweth of these things, before whom I speak freely; for I am persauded that none of these things are hidden from him; for this thing was not done in a corner. King Agrippa, believest thou the prophets? I know thou believest."

Almost Persuaded.

Then said Agrippa, "Almost thou persaudest me to be a Christian."

"I would to God," answered Paul, "That not only thou, but also all that hear me this day, were both almost and altogether such as I am, except these bonds."

Should Be Free.

After listening to Paul's great address, the king and his sister, and the governor withdrew to one side, and said that there was no cause to keep Paul a prisoner, for he had done nothing worthy of death or of bonds.

"This man," said Agrippa to Festus, "might have been set at liberty, if he had not appealed unto Caesar."

St. Paul at Miletus with the Elders of the Church at Ephesus
"And they all wept sore, and fell on Paul's neck, and kissed him, sorrowing most of all for the words which he spake, that they should see his face no more.

LESSON 37 THE VOYAGE TO ROME

"If we acknowledge God in all our ways, he has promised safely to direct our steps, and in our experience we shall find the promise fulfilled."

Julius the Roman Captain.

Paul's appeal to Caesar made it necessary for him to go to Rome, Italy, where the Roman Emperor lived. Accordingly, when all was in readiness, and passage on a ship secured, Paul and some other prisoners embarked for Rome. He was put into the charge of a Roman captain named Julius, a man who proved to be a kind, honorable gentleman, and a true friend to Paul. He recognized that his apostle-prisoner was a great and good man, and possessed wisdom superior to that even of the wisest. Thrilling experiences happened on this voyage that proved to Julius that Paul was not only wise but also inspired of the Lord. No matter where Paul was, in whose company he was thrown, in peace or persecution, in prospect of life or threatened death, he was always the same earnest preacher of the Gospel—a true servant of his Lord and Master Jesus Christ. This is why even his enemies respected and feared him, and why Julius and other honest men admired and loved him.

Companions.

On the Sea.

Two of Paul's true friends were with them, Luke the doctor and historian, and Aristarchus from Thessalonica. Sailing northward from Caesarea, they stopped for a day at Sidon, where, through the courtesy of Julius, Paul went ashore to see his friends who were living there. What a happy and yet sad meeting that must have been! From Sidon, they sailed to the northwest, past the island of Cyprus, thence westward, past the shore of Asia Minor. At Myra, a city of Lycia, Julius, the Centurion, found a ship sailing from Alexandria to Italy, so he transferred his prisoners from the ship of Adranythum to the one from Alexandria. This latter ship was loaded with wheat that was being taken from Egypt to Italy.

"The Fair Havens."

For many days, the ship moved very slowly because of a heavy wind, but at length it came to the island of Crete. They followed its shore until they found a harbor called "The Fair Havens," near the city of Lasea. As it was not a very good place in which to spend the winter, the owner concluded to sail to another harbor.

PAUL GIVES WARNING

As the sailing was dangerous, it being late in the season, Paul warned them not to leave, saying:

Inspired Warning.

"Sirs, I perceive that this voyage will be with injury and much damage, not only of the lading of the ship, but also of our lives;" and he urged them to stay where they were for the winter.

But the owner of the ship, believing Paul didn't know anything about sailing, said it was alright to go; and the Centurion believing the owner of the ship had better judgment than Paul, consented to sail for sea again.

Ancient Ships.

The ships in those days were not like the steamships of today. They were "rudely built and rigged; having one large mast, through whose head passed Ancient strong ropes; and one large sail. It was steered by two paddle-rudders. Easily strained and exposed to leakage, it was in danger of floundering; the way in which many ancient vessels were lost. Ropes were carried for binding the hull when weakened by storm. On the prow was a painted eye, as if seeking direction and watching against danger. Its ornaments were figures of heathen divinities, to whom idolatrous and superstitious sailors looked for protection."

Paul's judgment told him it was dangerous to attempt to cross the Mediterranean Sea in such a boat, and he knew by the inspiration of the Lord that, if the sailors attempted to do so, they would meet with disaster.

There were two hundred and seventy-six persons on board as they weighed anchor at Fair Havens, and continued their journey. The fair weather and favorable wind gave promise of a successful and safe voyage; and no doubt the sailors laughed at Paul for his fears.

A Storm Begins.

But suddenly all was changed. A strong wind sweeping down from the mountains on the shore, struck the ship and wheeled it around. The sailors were unable to control it, and the rudder was powerless to guide it. Behind the ship was a little boat, which they now pulled up on board; and as the ship was being threatened to be dashed to pieces, they bound it with ropes to keep it together, and if possible, to prevent it from leaking.

Ship Threatened.

But notwithstanding all their efforts, the boat began to leak, and was driven out into the sea. It was then that "they began to lighten the ship." Still the "tempestuous" wind and rain beat against the ship, and the danger of ship wreck increased every hour. The hours dragged on into days, and the hungry, stricken passengers and sailors paced terror-stricken day and night. On the third day, Luke says, "We cast out with our own hands the tackling of the ship;" by which we conclude that the ship was leaking so badly that even the passengers assisted in casting overboard everything that could be thrown.

"And when neither sun nor stars in many days appeared, and no small tempest lay on us, all hope that we should be saved was then taken away."

Even Luke, it seems lost heart, and was about to give up.

All in Despair but One.

"Without regular food—and what they had probably in a spoiled condition—drenched and cold, despair seized the whole company. But there was one exception—that was Paul. While others were losing hope, 'he was engaged in earnest prayer.' Neither discomfort nor danger, nor opposition to his counsels, nor these combined could disturb his calmness which was so unlike the fear and anguish about him. There was a great contrast between the reeling ship and his firmness; between the darkness, and the heavenly light within him; between bodily weakness and spiritual strength; between the despairing cries about him, and his calm voice; between the painted eye on the ship's prow, and the all-seeing eye upon him; between the ornamental images of powerless false gods, and the Almighty Ruler over all."

In the midst of this despair and darkness, Paul arose, and said:

A Prophecy.

"Sirs, ye should have hearkened unto me, and not have loosed from Crete, and to have gained this harm and loss. And now, I exhort you to be of good cheer: for there shall be no loss of any man's life among you, but the ship. For there stood by me this night the angel of God, whose I am, and whom I serve, saying, Fear not, Paul; thou must be brought before Caesar; and lo, God has given thee all of them that sail with thee; wherefore, sirs, be of good cheer; for I believe God, that it shall be even as it was told me. But we must be cast upon an island."

Sailors Attempt to Escape.

For fourteen days the storm lasted; and then one night the sailors thought they were nearing land. They sounded the depth and found the water twenty fathoms deep; then in a little while, they measured again, and found it fifteen fathoms deep, so they knew that land was not far away. They anchored the ship, and looked anxiously for the day. Then some of the sailors began to lower the little boat, pretending to throw out more anchors, but really intending to forsake the ship and leave all on board to destruction. When Paul discovered their purpose, he said to the Centurion,

Paul Stops Them.

"Unless these sailors stay in the ship none of us can be saved." At this the soldiers cut the rope and let the boat fall away, so the sailors could not get off.

Comfort and Food.

About daylight, Paul addressed the company again, and urged them to take food. "This is the fourteenth day," he said, "that you have gone without eating, wherefore, I pray you to take some meat; for this is for your health: for there shall not a hair fall from the head of any of you."

He then took bread, and gave thanks in the presence of them all: and when he had broken it, he began to eat. Encouraged by Paul's faith and assurance, they all broke their fast, and then lightened the ship by throwing overboard the wheat.

As soon as daylight came, they could see land, but did not know what place it was. However, they saw a creek coming into the sea, and concluded they could run their ship safely into the bay. So they cut anchor, hoisted the sail, and struck for shore.

As a climax of all disasters, the ship ran aground. The front end stuck fast in the sand and the rear part began to break in pieces.

Ship Wrecked.

There was a Roman law which said a soldier must take a prisoner's place if the soldier permitted the prisoner to escape; so the soldiers fearing the prisoners might swim ashore and escape asked the Centurion to kill all the prisoners while they were on board. But Julius, desiring to save Paul's life, refused to permit the prisoners to be killed. Some then swam ashore, and rendering help to others, succeeded in getting every soul safe to land—not one life was lost, but the ship, just as Paul had foretold it.

The island was Melita, just south of Sicily.

THE POWER OF GOD MANIFEST

Luke says "the barbarous people showed us no little kindness; for they kindled a fire, and received us everyone, because of the present rain, and because of the cold."

Bitten by a Viper.

Paul was busy helping to feed the fire, and to make it more comfortable for himself and others, when something happened that startled the natives. A viper crawled from one of the sticks, and fastened itself on Paul's hand. When the people saw it, and knew how poisonous it was, they said:

"No doubt this man is a murderer, whom, though he hath escaped the sea, yet vengeance will not permit to live."

Natives Astonished.

Then they looked for him to swell up and die. But they were surprised to see that not the least harm came to him. Then they changed their minds, and said he was a god.

Gospel Preached.

Undoubtedly, Paul told them who he was, and preached the Gospel of Jesus Christ to them. They were entertained by Publius, the chief man of the island, who also heard the Gospel, and saw the power of the Priesthood made manifest. His father was sick of fever, and very ill. Paul administered to him by laying on of hands, and he was instantly healed. The news of these miracles soon spread with the result that many who were sick "came to the brethren and were healed."

"All these honored us with many honors," says the historian Luke, "And when we departed, they loaded us with such things as were necessary."

Seeds of Truth Sown.

What a blessing to these people was the three months sojourn of Paul and his companions, and with what keen regret and sorrow they must have said goodby when the "Castor and Pollus," the ship from Alexandria, carried Paul away from them forever? It carried him, but not the truths he had taught. These would remain with them, and, if accepted, would bless them eternally.

LESSON 38 THE WORLD ENRICHED BY A PRISONER CHAINED

"The blood of the Martyrs is the seed of the Church."

Anticipation vs. Realization.

A few school boys, one day, met to debate the question, "Resolved, That there is more pleasure in Anticipation than in Realization." One on the side that tried to prove that Anticipation gives more pleasure, referred to every boy's experience at Christmas time, saying that the day before Christmas and Christmas Eve always give more joy than Christmas itself—"As soon as the boy gets his toys, then he begins to regret that Christmas isn't tomorrow."

That boy expressed in his simple way about the same thought contained in this sentence from Emerson: "Man looks forward with smiles but backward with sighs;" or as another writer puts it, "What we expect is always greater than what we enjoy."

Such may not be the case always in life; but it certainly must have been Paul's experience in regard to his anticipated visit to Rome. For several years he had looked forward with pleasure to the time when he would have the opportunity to preach the Gospel in the famous capital of the great Roman Empire. But now as he approaches the realization of his hopes, he is an old man, worn with exposure and confinement, and a prisoner.

However, we must not conclude that he was left comfortless, or that he had any less desire to bear testimony to the world of the divine mission of his Savior. On the contrary he continued to seize every opportunity to preach the everlasting Gospel.

Syracuse.

This he did when the "Castor and Pollux" or "The Twin Brothers," stopped eighty miles north from Malta, at a place called Syracuse, the ancient capital of Sicily. It is not unlikely that Paul asked permission to go ashore and preach the Gospel to the Jews and the Gentiles who were in that celebrated city. If so, we are sure Julius would grant his request. At any rate, the Sicilians afterward claimed that Paul founded the Church on that island.

Puteoli.

His next important stop was on the northern part of the beautiful bay of Naples, where was situated a town named Puteoli; now known as *Pozzuoli.* As the ship carrying Paul and his friends entered this harbor, it was met by a crowd of people who had gathered to greet it. Among these were "brethren" who came to welcome and comfort the missionary-prisoner. Perhaps through a desire of Julius to remain here long enough to communicate with Rome, or it may be through his kindness to Paul, the company remained at Puteoli seven days, thus giving the Elders an opportunity to spend a Sabbath day with the Saints in that place. How refreshing to Paul's spirit to worship once again with those who possessed the same testimony of the Gospel as he!

Met by True Friends.

Word having been sent ahead that Paul was on his way from Puteoli to Rome, many of the brethren in that city started out to meet the beloved and famous missionary. No doubt the Saints in Rome realized that Paul's spirit as well as his body would be worn and weary, and, as true friends indeed, they made preparation to go to him. True friendship always prompts one to go to a friend in adversity rather than in prosperity. It may be that they desired only to give him a royal convoy into their city; for he was truly a royal personage even though bound in chains. Whatever their motive, some of the brethren traveled forty-one miles, and met their beloved Apostle at the Apii Forum. Another party met him at "Three Taverns"—thirty miles from Rome. Paul's heart was touched by this manifestation of friendship and true brotherhood, and he "thanked God, and took courage."

Under Guard.

When the company reached the renowned capital of the ancient world, it must have seemed to Paul like a huge prison; and when his friends parted from him to go to their own homes and he to his guarded place, his heart must have been heavy indeed. However, Julius kindly delivered his prisoner over to the captain of the Pretorian Guard, the highest military authority in the city—the guard that had charge of all those who were to come before the Emperor for trial. Fortunately, Paul was not put in prison but permitted to dwell in a house by himself, under the constant guard of a soldier. Here he was given all the freedom possible, to a prisoner; so, true to his energetic spirit, he found many opportunities to continue his preaching. This he would do first to the soldiers to whom he was chained daily. As they would frequently relieve one another, he would have ample opportunity to preach the truth to many of the guards, and thus, probably, indirectly to the Emperor himself.

Appeals to Jews.

He made occasion, also, to preach to the Jews. He called the chief men of this nation together and told them why he was then a prisoner. "Though I have committed nothing against the people, or customs of our fathers," said he, "yet was I delivered prisoner from Jerusalem into the hands of the Romans, who, when they had examined me, would have let me go, because there was no cause of death in me; but when the Jews spake against it, I was constrained to appeal unto Caesar.

"For this cause therefore have I called for you, to see you, and to speak with you, because that for the hope of Israel I am bound with this chain."

Jews Reject Message.

The Jews answered that they had heard nothing of evil against him; but "as concerning this sect (meaning the Christians), we know that everywhere it is spoken against." In fact, in Rome as elsewhere, the Jews rejected the Gospel message, and compelled Paul to turn to the Gentiles.

The Gospel Spreads.

For nearly eight hundred days, Paul remained a prisoner awaiting his trial before the Emperor. During that time, he preached the Gospel to hundreds of soldiers who had one after another daily been appointed as guards. These, when converted, would convert others, and when sent off to Roman provinces, would spread the Gospel in new lands, thus widening the area in which the light of truth might shine.

Message Through Epistles.

But that was not the only way in which it radiated from the humble abode of the missionary-prisoner. During that two years confinement, he kept in communication with the Church in Europe and Asia. As there were no railroads, no steamboats, nor telegraph, every letter that he received or that he sent to them was carried by a courier, who had to travel very slowly by land and sea, sometimes for hundreds of miles. But he had loving friends attending him who were always ready to bear his messages. Some of these you already know. Luke, the faithful physician; Timothy, his son in the Gospel; John Mark, who, you remember, started with Paul and Barnabas on their first mission; Aristarchus of Thessalonica; Epaphroditus, a friend from Macedonia; Onesimus, a slave belonging to Paul's friend, Philemon, and others. With these faithful servants as messengers,

Paul wrote letters, called epistles, which have made the whole world better and richer in the knowledge of truth. These letters are now in the New Testament, and are called Epistle to the Philippians, Epistles to Philemon, Epistle to the Colossians, and Epistle to the Ephesians.

Thus did Paul's epistles written in a Roman prison become literally "Winged messengers that can fly from east to west on embassies of love."

Released.

Certainty of what Paul did after his having been a prisoner in Rome for two years, ends with Luke's statement, that he "received all that came unto him, preaching the kingdom of God, and teaching those things which concern the Lord Jesus Christ with all confidence, no man forbidding him." It is believed, however, that he was finally given his liberty and that he preached in many lands, tradition saying that he even went to England. It is thought that it was during this missionary tour that he wrote his first letter to Timothy, who had been appointed to take care of the church at Ephesus, and also the one to Titus who was with the churches on the island of Crete.

Again Arrested.

About the year 64 A. D., however, he was again arrested and imprisoned in Rome. Only a year previous the Saints had been persecuted to death by the wicked Nero. They had been thrown into the Arena, devoured by wild beasts, burned to death as human torches, and martyred in other cruel ways.

Beheaded.

It was soon after the burning of Rome by this wicked emperor, that Paul, the most energetic of all missionaries, after thirty years of constant service in the ministry, was put to death by beheading. Just before the end came, he wrote to Timothy these beautiful and pathetic words:

"I am now ready to be offered, and the time of my departure is at hand. I have fought a good fight, I have finished my course, I have kept the faith; henceforth there is laid up for me a crown of righteousness, which the Lord, the righteous judge, shall give me at that day.'"

As he bowed his head to receive the fatal stroke, we know that he could have said in very truth:

"I feel my immortality o'ersweep all pains, all tears, all time, all fears; and peal, like the eternal thunders of the deep, into my ears this truth—thou livest forever!"

Before the Royal he was kingly,
    In the prison, noble, true;
In the tempest, mighty captain
    Of a terror-stricken crew.

Sunless days nor nights of blackness,
    Prison chains—tempestuous wave.
Floundered ship nor deadly viper—
    Feared he not the yawning grave.

"God's good angel stood beside me,
    His I am and Him I serve,"
This the secret of his power—
    Him from Right no power could swerve.

ST. PAUL.
Chained by the wrist to his soldier guard, in his own house, for two whole years.

The Meaning of Life and Other Useless Crap is perhaps our generations greatest work as it answers the age old question "What is the meaning of life?" Written simply and straightforward it is easy to understand why Ben Lemon is the most important living philosopher. It hasn't been since A Modest Proposal that a pamphlet can our perceptions so dramatically.

Made in the USA
San Bernardino, CA
09 July 2019